# GREATEST GARDEN

## ART IN PROFILE

Michele Hardy, Curator, Nickle Galleries, University of Calgary
ISSN 1700-9995 (Print) ISSN 1927-4351 (Online)

The Art in Profile series showcases the meaningful contributions of Canadian artists and architects, both emerging and established. Each book provides insight into the life and work of an artist or architect who asserts creativity, individuality, and cultural identity.

No.  1 · *Ancestral Portraits: The Colour of My People* | Frederick R. McDonald

No.  2 · *Magic off Main: The Art of Esther Warkov* | Beverly J. Rasporich

No.  3 · *The Garden of Art: Vic Cicansky, Sculptor* | Don Kerr

No.  5 · *Reta Summers Cowley* | Terry Fenton

No.  6 · *Spirit Matters: Ron (Gyo-Zo) Spickett, Artist, Poet, Lay-Priest* | Geoffrey Simmins

No.  7 · *Full Spectrum: The Architecture of Jeremy Sturgess* | Edited by Geoffrey Simmins

No.  8 · *Cultural Memories and Imagined Futures: The Art of Jane Ash Poitras* | Pamela McCallum

No.  9 · *The Art of John Snow* | Elizabeth Herbert

No. 10 · *Cover and Uncover: Eric Cameron* | Edited by Ann Davis

No. 11 · *Marion Nicoll: Silence and Alchemy* | Ann Davis and Elizabeth Herbert

No. 12 · *John C. Parkin, Archives, and Photography: Reflections on the Practice and Presentation of Modern Architecture* | Linda Fraser, Michael McMordie, and Geoffrey Simmins

No. 13 · *From Realism to Abstraction: The Art of J. B. Taylor* | Adriana A. Davies

No. 14 · *The Writing on the Wall: The Work of Joane Cardinal-Schubert* | Edited by Lindsey V. Sharman

No. 15 · *Greatest Garden: The Paintings of David More* | Mary-Beth Laviolette

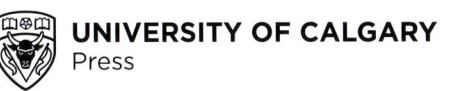

**UNIVERSITY OF CALGARY**
Press

# Greatest Garden
## The Paintings of DAVID MORE

**MARY-BETH LAVIOLETTE**

Art in Profile Series
ISSN 1700-9995 (Print) ISSN 1927-4351 (Online)

University of Calgary Press
2500 University Drive NW
Calgary, Alberta
Canada T2N 1N4
press.ucalgary.ca

LIBRARY AND ARCHIVES CANADA CATALOGUING IN PUBLICATION

Title: Greatest garden : the paintings of David More / Mary-Beth Laviolette.
Other titles: Paintings of David More
Names: Laviolette, Mary-Beth, author. | Container of (work): More, Dave.
  Paintings. Selections.
Series: Art in profile ; 15.
Description: Series statement: Art in profile, ISSN (print) 1700-9995, ISSN
  (ebook) 1927-4351 ; no. 15 | Includes bibliographical references.
Identifiers: Canadiana (print) 20210217529 | Canadiana (ebook) 20210217618
  | ISBN 9781773852249 (softcover) | ISBN 9781773852256 (Open Access PDF) |
  ISBN 9781773852263 (PDF) | ISBN 9781773852270 (EPUB)
Subjects: LCSH: More, Dave. | LCSH: More, Dave—Criticism and interpretation.
  | LCSH: Painting, Canadian—Alberta—20th century. | LCSH: Painters—
  Alberta—Biography. | LCSH: Gardens in art. | LCGFT: Biographies.
Classification: LCC ND249.M5773 L38 2021 | DDC 759.11—dc23

The University of Calgary Press acknowledges the support of the Government of Alberta through the Alberta Media Fund for our publications. We acknowledge the financial support of the Government of Canada. We acknowledge the financial support of the Canada Council for the Arts for our publishing program.

This book has been published with the support of the Red Deer Museum + Art Gallery.

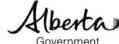 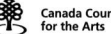 

Printed and bound in Canada by Friesens
♻ This book is printed on Garda Matt Art paper

Copyediting by Brian Scrivener
Cover design, page design, and typesetting by Melina Cusano

# Contents

Strength and the Room to Dream     VI

Foreword     VII

Artist's Acknowledgements     IX

Introduction     1

1 | Benhaven Garden     13

2 | Local Wanderings (Near & Afar)     25

3 | Ghostly Forests, Uncertain Skies     47

4 | The Ignition of Memory, Part One: The Garden Ceremony     65

5 | The Ignition of Memory, Part Two: Canadian Window     83

Epilogue     101

Notes     102

## *Strength and the Room to Dream*

In 1977, a remarkable young woman came into my life.

She was insightful, energetic, empathic, humorous, intuitive, bold. She was beautiful and had a deliciously fiery temper. She was also a skilled photographer with an uncanny sense of pictorial design. I was smitten. Her name: Yvette Brideau. I asked her if she would like to come on an art adventure with me and see where it might lead our lives. She said yes. We both left our safe jobs and set off into the unpredictable.

Along the way, Yvette introduced me to a part of Canada I'd not experienced and to the unique culture of Acadian New Brunswick. We painted and photographed, we made drawings, we met and worked with filmmakers and television crews and authors and publishers, illustrated and wrote articles and books, painted murals and designed monuments, and met remarkable people. We lived in Calgary and on Vancouver Island and returned to Red Deer for ten years, and in 1994 we moved to Benalto. There we made a garden named Benhaven that became our ultimate artwork.

While my name might be on many of the pieces of art that come out of our adventure, without Yvette's input and spirit and devotion they might not even exist. Yvette brings the order and sensibility that is the foundation of our collaboration. She gives me what every creative person needs: strength and the room to dream.

Dave More

## Foreword

As Red Deer's cultural scene grows and matures, it is important to build a record of those who have made the path, inspired us, and used their creative talent to expand our perception of the world around us. Dave More's quiet passion for art, painting, and the natural landscape has been a longstanding inspiration for many artists and art lovers in this community. Through his teaching, his engagement with our arts organizations, as well as his deep engagement with his own practice as a painter, Dave More has made a lasting and inspiring impact on our community. Dave's joy in painting is infectious. When he invited Valerie Miller, the Red Deer Museum + Art Gallery's Curator of Collections, and me out to his studio in Benalto on a beautiful spring day in 2018, we thought he wanted to show us a new series of works for an exhibition. After showing us through his studio, and through Yvette's wonderful gardens, Dave invited us to sit down and hear his proposition: he wanted to donate his life's work to the Red Deer Museum + Art Gallery! We had begun a collection of works by Central Alberta artists, and Dave's generous offer would become the focal point for building our collection. His generosity and his confidence in us to care for his works moved me to tears.

When we presented an exhibition of Dave's magnificent works from his *Garden Ceremony* series in 2012, we invited Mary-Beth Laviolette to be our guest curator. She and Dave had an immediate affinity, and we benefitted from Mary-Beth's extensive knowledge of Alberta artists. With Dave's consent, we invited Mary-Beth to assist us in selecting works that would be representative of Dave's entire career as a painter. We spent days with Dave in his studio, looking at each work and making the seemingly impossible decisions about which ones to add to our collection. We chose 200 works and brought them all to the Red Deer Museum + Art Gallery in 2019.

Mary-Beth curated an exhibition, *Dave More: A Painter's Gift*, to showcase some of the works in the gift, and this book is the culmination of the inspiring journey that began that day in the garden. It has been extraordinary to work with Dave and Mary-Beth, and to listen in on their discussions about art and inspiration and landscape. It has been inspiring and a bit overwhelming to see all the works together, and now to see a publication that will make Dave's painting and his beliefs about his craft accessible to a broader audience.

The Red Deer Museum + Art Gallery is very grateful to the Community Initiatives Program of the Government of Alberta, the City of Red Deer, and the Alberta Foundation for the Arts for providing the funding that has enabled us to realize our vision for this project. I would also like to thank Joanne Gruenberg and Pat Matheson, the Red Deer Museum + Art Gallery's Curators of Art, and Kim Verrier, Exhibitions Coordinator, for their hard work in realizing all aspects of this project.

On behalf of the Board of the Red Deer Museum + Art Gallery, I am pleased to extend our sincere thanks to Dave More and Yvette Brideau for believing in us and entrusting us with such a precious legacy.

Lorna Johnson
Executive Director
Red Deer Museum + Art Gallery
March 24, 2021

## Artist's Acknowledgements

I first met Mary-Beth Laviolette in the early 1980s. She was a fresh young writer–a reporter for CBC radio–who came to do a story on our recently constructed Burns Visual Arts Society studios located in an old furniture warehouse above Stephen Avenue in downtown Calgary. As the janitor/treasurer of the group, I may have been the only one in the seventeen studios that afternoon, so she was stuck with interviewing me. What quickly impressed me was how astute she was. Her questions came from different angles than one would expect. I had to sit up and pay attention. I remember thinking afterwards, "She's very serious about the arts and their impact. She'll go far."

And has she ever.

Mary-Beth has become a legend in Canadian culture: a renowned curator of exhibitions, a valued historian, and an author of monumental proportions. She has an uncanny skill at wading through mounds of material and coming out the other side with the essence of it all. Her ability to perceive the ascending order of things is a remarkable talent that she has honed well. Her massive tome *An Alberta Art Chronicle: Adventures in Recent and Contemporary Art*, published in 2005, was the result of nearly ten years of concentrated research and compilation which set the benchmark for all reference work in the field of Alberta's visual arts. Over the years I have had the good fortune to have Mary-Beth curate two major exhibits of my work for the Red Deer MAG. To have her choose to write *Greatest Garden* is the deepest honour I could receive. In the years since that first meeting in my Calgary studio, our acquaintance has grown from one of earnest professionalism to one of warm and enduring friendship.

Without Lorna Johnson this book would not exist. Lorna's support of the visual arts in all their forms has been one of the signatures of her seventeen-year tenure as Executive Director of the Red Deer Museum + Art Gallery. Her ability to form the *long view* of a complex institution that combines museum with art gallery and all related programs has resulted in a first-rate organization with an enviable record. Under Lorna's vision I have benefited from two major exhibitions over the last decade, both shaped by the guiding hands of Mary-Beth. When it was suggested that a book might be forthcoming and that Mary-Beth would write it, I was astounded at the thought. To learn that the esteemed University of Calgary Press had agreed to the project has left me overwhelmed.

Under Lorna's leadership and Mary-Beth's curatorial vision the exhibits that led to *Greatest Garden* were handed to the masterful staff at Red Deer MAG: curators Joanne Gruenberg and Pat Matheson, exhibitions coordinator Kim Verrier, lighting expert Melanie Berndt, and communications whiz Karli Kendall, among others. The indomitable Dwight Arthur, who quietly and calmly photographed the images in this book left me spellbound with his skills, undaunted by what I considered impossible problems of massive paintings in far too small spaces.

I especially thank my *plein air* buddy Larry Reese, whose infectious enthusiasm for the challenge of painting outdoors remains a joy. Beneath all kinds of scenarios, be they storm-crossed or smoke-filled, Larry rises and challenges me to the timeless call of the sketchbook and easel. Our deep gratitude goes to our dear friend Ron Glover, without whom Benhaven would not have been realized. To our Family and Friends, thank you for your forever encouragement and support.

David More

# INTRODUCTION

## *"We come and go, guests of this Greatest garden."*

DAVID MORE (*The Garden Ceremony*)

*Greatest Garden*, featuring nearly sixty works of art by David More, is about one artist's sense of wonderment: a fascination and even an obsession with what has enraptured and, on occasion, alarmed him. This wonderment is located largely in the subject of the garden and its many wider associations – not just with what we grow but also with what thrives, decays, and perishes in wilder terrains. Spiritually, too, the garden can provide a kind of soulful sustenance, a place of refuge, as More and many others before him have experienced.

The most common description attached to David More is 'landscape artist'. This is true, but with subject matter that at times flows in different directions from the Canadian tradition of landscape as once defined by Tom Thomson, The Group of Seven, and Emily Carr. It begins the moment More steps out of his church studio in Benalto, Alberta, and walks back to his home through an expansive garden of shrubs, trees, and perennial flower beds.

Occupying almost two-thirds of a half-acre property, this sanctuary has been christened Benhaven Garden. It is the hands-on creation of Yvette Brideau, photographer and spouse. It is, as the opening chapter will show, a verdant subject for David. But his ideas about gardens do not stop there. Beyond the small hamlet of Benalto there is the fertile environment of Central Alberta, where the Scottish-born More (b. 1947) first arrived as a toddler and experienced the

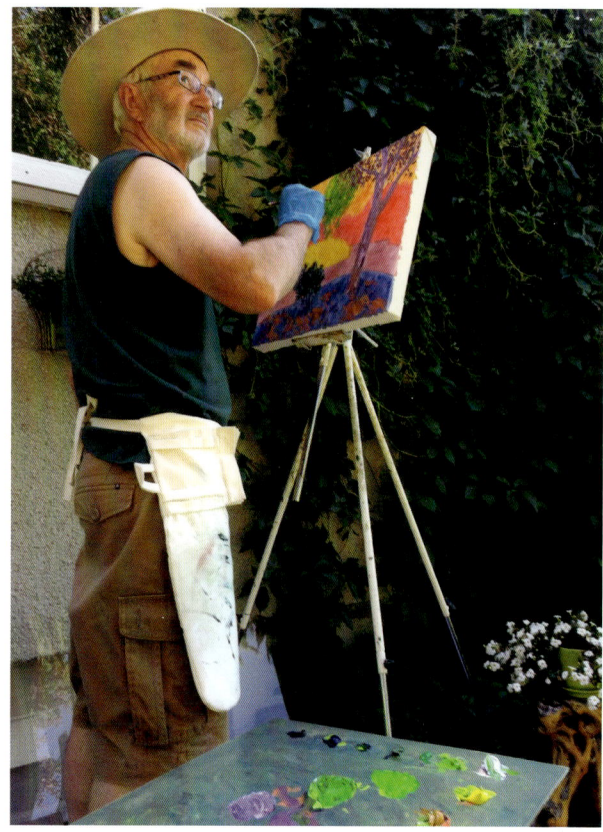

Artist in Benhaven Garden, July 2019
Photo credit: Yvette Brideau

comforting confines of an overgrown garden. Filed away in his memory bank are palpable images of its pastures, fields, forests, and smaller rivers flowing through the Parkland ecosystem.

During his nearly fifty years of practice, other sites of green enchantment have also encompassed Vancouver Island, India's formal gardens, and, from Yvette's Acadien homeland, the forests and wild shorelines of northern New Brunswick. Each place left a deep impression on the painter far beyond its scenic value. Noticeable, too, is the presence, either physically or implied, of the human subject. For More, his art encompasses two interwoven themes–the natural and the human landscape.[1]

A garden or a cultivated landscape for More is a reflection of the human condition and "a metaphor of man's timeless will to be in control of his environment, no matter how large or small."[2] But, sometimes, this ageless impulse leads thoughtlessly to a destructive rather than a creative relationship. In "Ghostly Forests, Uncertain Skies," a chapter related to climate change, are some of the earliest *exhibited* works of Canadian art I am aware of about this concern. It began when More, the young artist and forest wanderer, came in contact with the impact of acid rain on the forests of New Brunswick. Executed with a dramatic and discordant colour range, *Forest–Fade to Silent* (1990)–a breakthrough series of national consequence–left no doubt about the poisoning of a wilderness environment that is part of More's greater garden.

Raised and educated in Red Deer, Alberta, More received formal training from 1968-1972 at the Alberta College of Art (now Alberta University of the Arts).[3] As an artist interested in drawing and painting, but not without curiosity about other more experimental means, such as mixed media and the use of film negatives on canvas and wood,[4] More graduated in Fine Art with a major in Painting.

From there, setting the stage for further development as a figurative artist, came work as a graphic artist in the Faculty of Medicine at the University of Calgary and the beginnings of a habit now almost fifty years old: outdoor oil sketches. Notably, also sown were the seeds for the series *Garden Ceremony*, with large abstracted mixed media images derived from personal research carried out in Calgary and in other countries.

The 1970s were heady years for many a young artist of More's generation. In his case, there was sessional teaching at ACA, a Canada Council for the Arts grant, exhibit

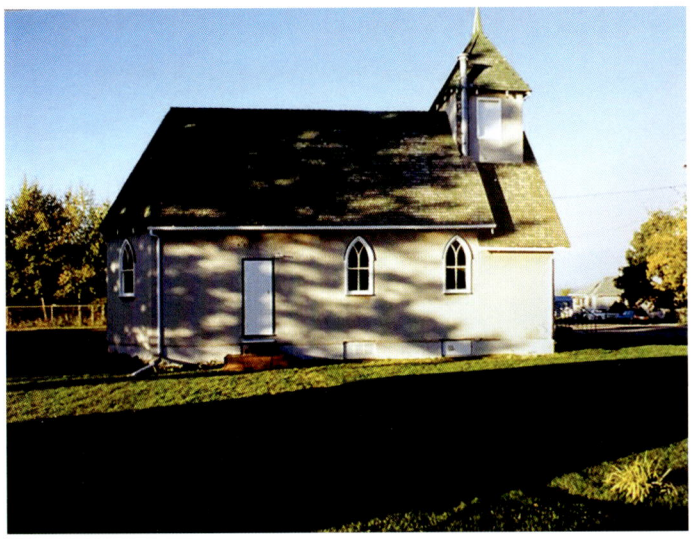

Benalto Presbyterian church purchased in 1994 by David More & Yvette Brideau
Photo credit: Yvette Brideau

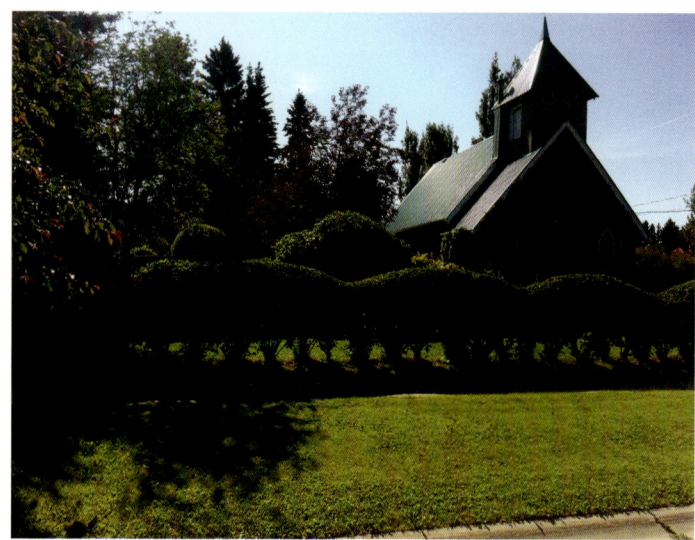

David More's Benalto Studio Today
Photo credit: Yvette Brideau

opportunities in public art galleries in Winnipeg, Edmonton, and Calgary, and his first solo show of acrylic paintings inspired by the mountainous and mined Crowsnest Pass region at the University of Calgary in 1979. In the world of book illustration, there was work, too, for the well-rounded artist. Through Edmonton's ambitious Hurtig Publishers came a five-book collaboration with humourist Eric Nicol. Later, for Red Deer Press and author Rudy Wiebe, there were his colourful Group of Seven-influenced paintings for the Canadian classic *Chinook Christmas* (1992). More also threw energy into co-founding the Burns Visual Arts Society, a co-op of artist studios first housed in the historic Burns Building in downtown Calgary.[5] As the decade ended, he made his first journey to New Brunswick with then-girlfriend Yvette Brideau.

Throughout this formative period, the shaping of More's artistic personality found nourishment from his studio training at the Calgary-based art college. From the Penticton-born art instructor George Angliss, More gained a solid foundation in classical painting and an all-important introduction to landscape art. From painter Frank Vervoort, he learned drawing and anatomy, while two years of sculpture with Olle Holmsten, an accomplished creator of commissioned public art, sharpened More's appreciation for three-dimensional form. Another lively addition to the art college's roster was the young Harold Feist, then at the start of an illustrious career as a painter. The Texas-born Feist exposed More to an edgier American point of view that feasted on colour, energy, and pure abstraction.

Good advice lasting a lifetime also came from George Wood, an early advocate of a then-novel medium: acrylic paint. Painting for More was and is a visceral adventure with colour, especially the kind applied by brush or palette knife as a thick, luscious pigment: colour against colour, over top, within, and under. There was, in other words, wonderment to be had in the process of painting–whether witnessed through the expressive energies of Tom Thomson and The Group of Seven or, more recently, Les Automatiste Jean-Paul Riopelle. But, "an avalanche of brushstrokes, laden with intense and powerful colours"[6] (as the artist described it) was not completely satisfying. Thankfully, from Wood came the suggestion to try an opposite approach involving thin veils of acrylic stain.

It was a breakthrough for More, enabling him to "evolve an approach to paint that allowed me to share the beautiful delicacy inherent in thin washes with a combination

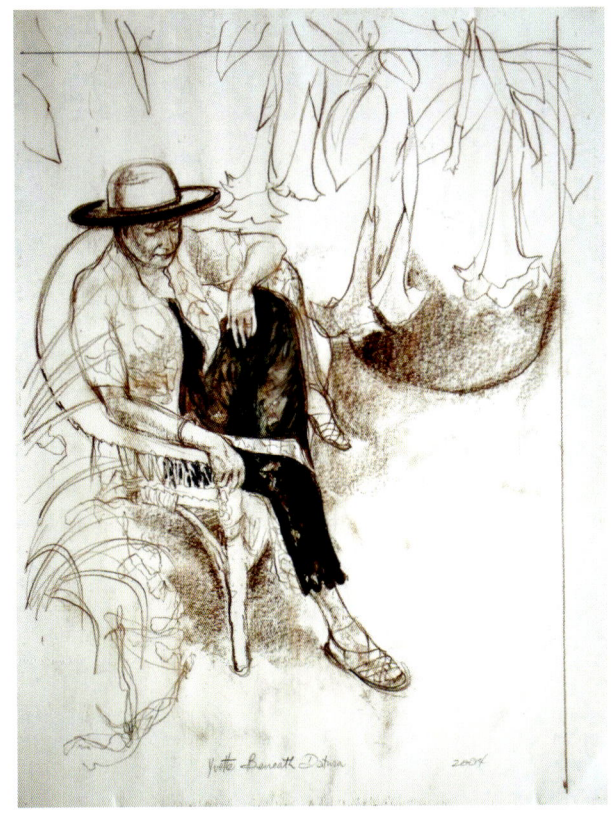

David More. *Yvette Beneath Daturas* (Majak Greenhouse), 2004, conté chalk on paper
Photo credit: Yvette Brideau

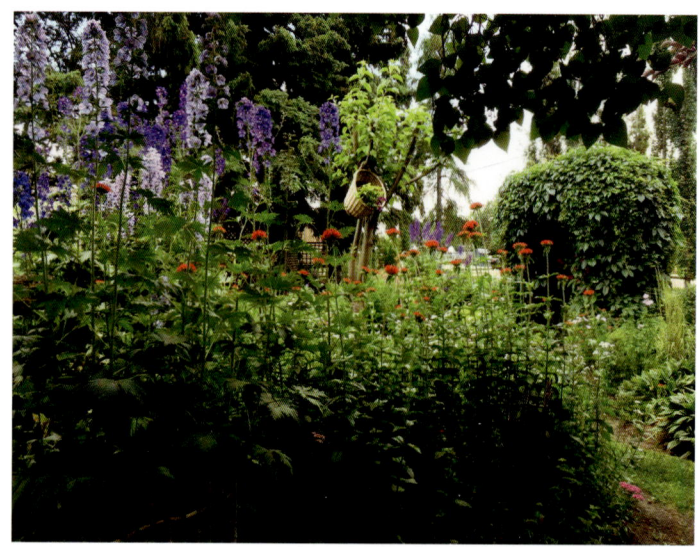

Inside the Memory Garden (Benhaven Garden), 2017
Photo credit: Yvette Brideau

of overplayed thick impasto [in oil]."[7] This practice is most evident in his *Canadian Window* series, where family and friends in a domestic interior are portrayed in acrylic, while behind them the landscape present in the large picture window is painted in oil. The result is a tricky union between two media which technically could not be more different in their makeup. But, in *Canadian Windows*, the crisp and controlled edges of the interiors and their human subjects contrast amicably with the textural and glossier surfaces of the exterior scene--a kind of yin and yang in picture-making.

Largely instinctive, it seems, more than the result of diligent training, More's drawing reaches expressive heights with graphite or charcoal on paper and mixed media works of coloured pencil and oil pastel. (A few of my personal favourites are the pencil studies for the *Canadian Window* series in Chapter 5 and the striking charcoals of forest decay – *Infusion/Forest,* featured in Chapter 3.) There is the strong imprint of memory, too. Elusive, fleeting, and never the same, sometimes photographs and sketches are involved in the process of making a work of art. Essentially melded together in one image are the real and the imagined. This is evident particularly in More's ongoing *Garden*

*Ceremony* series, which has accompanied him since the late 1970s. Several iterations of this theme are presented in Chapter 4's *The Ignition of Memory: Garden Ceremony*.

An art instructor at Red Deer College for nearly thirty years, David More is part of a lively community of artists who call central Alberta home, its artistic development not as widely recognized as other centres such as Edmonton, Calgary, and Lethbridge. Too many to be comprehensively listed, there are the award-winning ceramic creations of Trudy Golley, Pat Matheson, Shirley Rimer, and Robin Lambert; the textile works of Matt Gould addressing gender and sexuality; the intricate glass art of Darren and Deborah Petersen; the comic-book-style wood engravings and drawings of Jim Westergard; the impressive Powwow regalia of artists and curators Patrick and Marissa (Mocassin) Mitsuing, and, on a much smaller scale, the Punk/Goth inspired miniatures of Jason Frizzell. More, nonetheless, has an active record of exhibitions in both public and commercial art galleries: around thirty-three solo and group exhibitions in Alberta and beyond.

In the wider context of western Canadian landscape art, More shares artistic terrain with three other artists of a similar age, artistic temperament, and commitment to

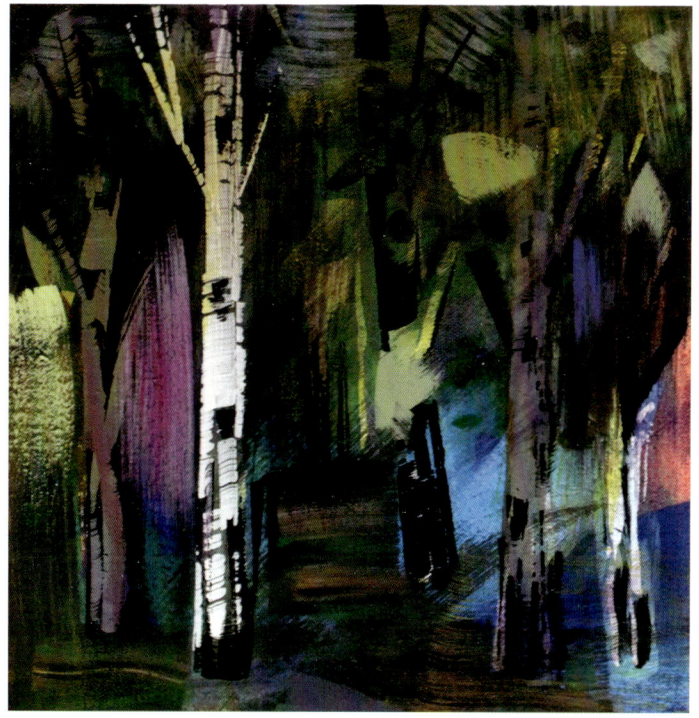

Barbara Ballachey, *Forest Light*, 2017
Acrylic on canvas, 10 x 10 inches (25.4 x 25.4 cm)
Photo credit: The Edge Gallery, Canmore AB

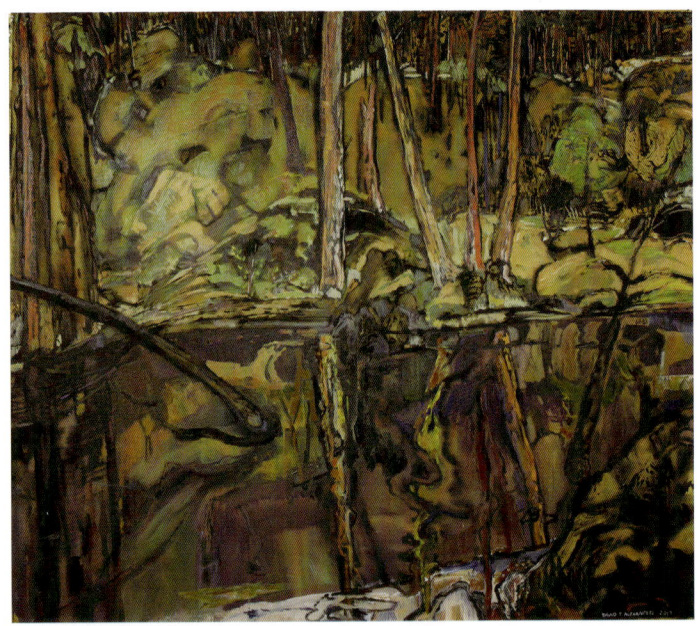

David Alexander, *Drawn from the Night Pool*, 2017
Acrylic on canvas, 57 x 66 inches (144.78 x 167.64 cm)
Photo credit: Peter Robertson Gallery, Edmonton AB

the expressive image. Rather than an accurate depiction of place, feeling or emotion are more pertinent. They are David Alexander (b. 1947, Vancouver), Barbara Ballachey (b. 1949, Edmonton), and Gregory Hardy (b. 1950, Saskatoon). All four developed artistic practices in the early 1970s, with Alexander, Ballachey, and More receiving post-secondary art training during the generous years of institutional and art gallery expansion in western Canada. Greg Hardy is considered self-developed with many excursions made to the two-week summer workshops of Emma Lake, Saskatchewan. Organized by the Kenderdine Campus (University of Saskatchewan) and founded in 1955, Emma Lake was a site of artistic pilgrimage.[8] For those inspired by contemporary landscape, modern art, and abstraction, there was no other artist residency during its time, more widely regarded in the Canadian art world.[9] On the roster of workshop participants, the names of Alexander, Ballachey, and Hardy appear often to paint, instruct, and inspire.[10]

David More, on the other hand, then based in Calgary, found additional sustenance through travel. There was his research of garden imagery in Rio de Janeiro, Britain, and France–beginning to take shape as the *Garden Ceremony* in the late 1970s–and further travel to Boston and New

Brunswick, followed by two years on Vancouver Island where some of the subjects for his *Canadian Window* series first emerged. The Island is also where his first outdoor mural commission was unveiled.[11]

Exploring methodically the different terrains of western Canada, we can read about how David Alexander is a dedicated backcountry explorer, more recently involving the desert-like southern Okanagan.[12] There is also Barbara Ballachey's preoccupation with the rolling foothills of western Alberta, Gregory Hardy's devotion to the prairies and lakes of Saskatchewan, and David More's own explorations locally and further afield. In common, their art is laden with the *experience* of place, light, and weather. Critical to all their development is the influence of not just Canadian landscape art as expressed earlier in Tom Thomson's innovative oil sketches but also in later, postwar abstraction. Colour-field painting, with its preference for large areas of flat, solid colour, is particularly evident with Ballachey's lyrical and abstracted treatment of the land.

Of the four, More is the only one who has dealt with the human subject (*Canadian Windows, Shore Figures Sylvan Lake*) and what people have created and altered, examples being the *Garden Ceremony* and *Benhaven Garden* series.

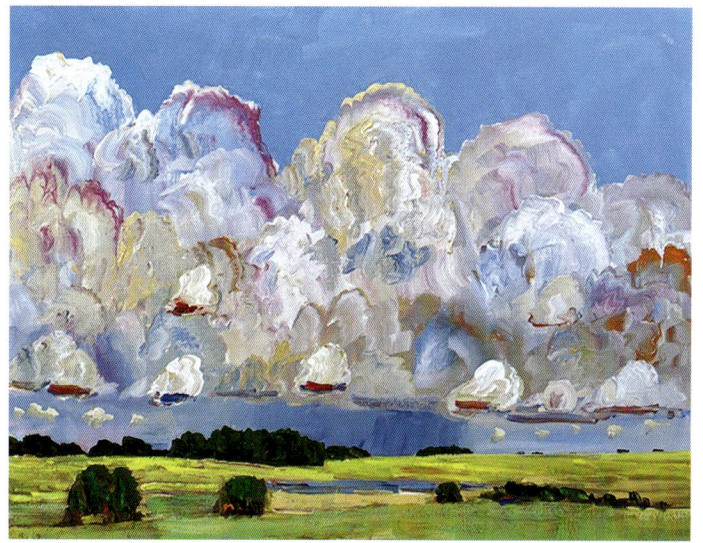

Greg Hardy, *To The West*, 2020
Acrylic on canvas, 38 x 48 inches (96.52 x 121.92 cm)

In that case, his art is largely representational. As for his approach to the environment, abstraction plays a larger role, executed by the more vigorous and expressive brushwork seen in *Fade to Silent* and *Infusion/Forest*.

Alexander, Ballachey, Hardy, and More are all colourists with bold, heightened interpretations of nature and its various forms. Colour is easily exaggerated for emotional effect. There is also a physicality and texture apparent in their process of applying paint which More first experienced in his years as an art student. For him, it is indeed a version of the aforementioned "avalanche" but practised in a more disciplined manner where the infusion with different colours, both light and dark, play and dance on a coloured ground.

• • • • • • • • •

The paintings and works on paper represented in *Greatest Garden* derive from a generous gift the artist made to the Red Deer & District Museum Society Art Collection in 2018. This donation was followed by a retrospective look at his contribution to Canadian art titled *David More: A Painter's Gift*. Serving as the curator for this exhibition, which was on view at the gallery from October 12, 2019 to January 1, 2020, I selected many of the pieces reproduced now in *Greatest Garden*. Overall, there were many pathways to follow in representing the diversity of themes that have preoccupied the artist over the last fifty years. Not all stages of the artist's development are covered, but I felt More's attachment to central Alberta was particularly important to stress. This included prairie and parkland, people at rest in their homes and on a nearby popular beach.

But More's impressions are not just reflective of a sense of place; they are also environmental and philosophical–concerned with the human condition or existence. Much of this has wrapped itself around the notion of the garden, either wild or lovingly cultivated, expressed in the wonderful medium of paint and its charcoal and mixed media accomplices.

In aiding with this exploration, my gratitude goes to David and Yvette as well as Red Deer Museum + Art Gallery's executive director, Lorna Johnson, and curatorial staff, Joanne Gruenberg and Pat Matheson.

Mary-Beth Laviolette, January 2021

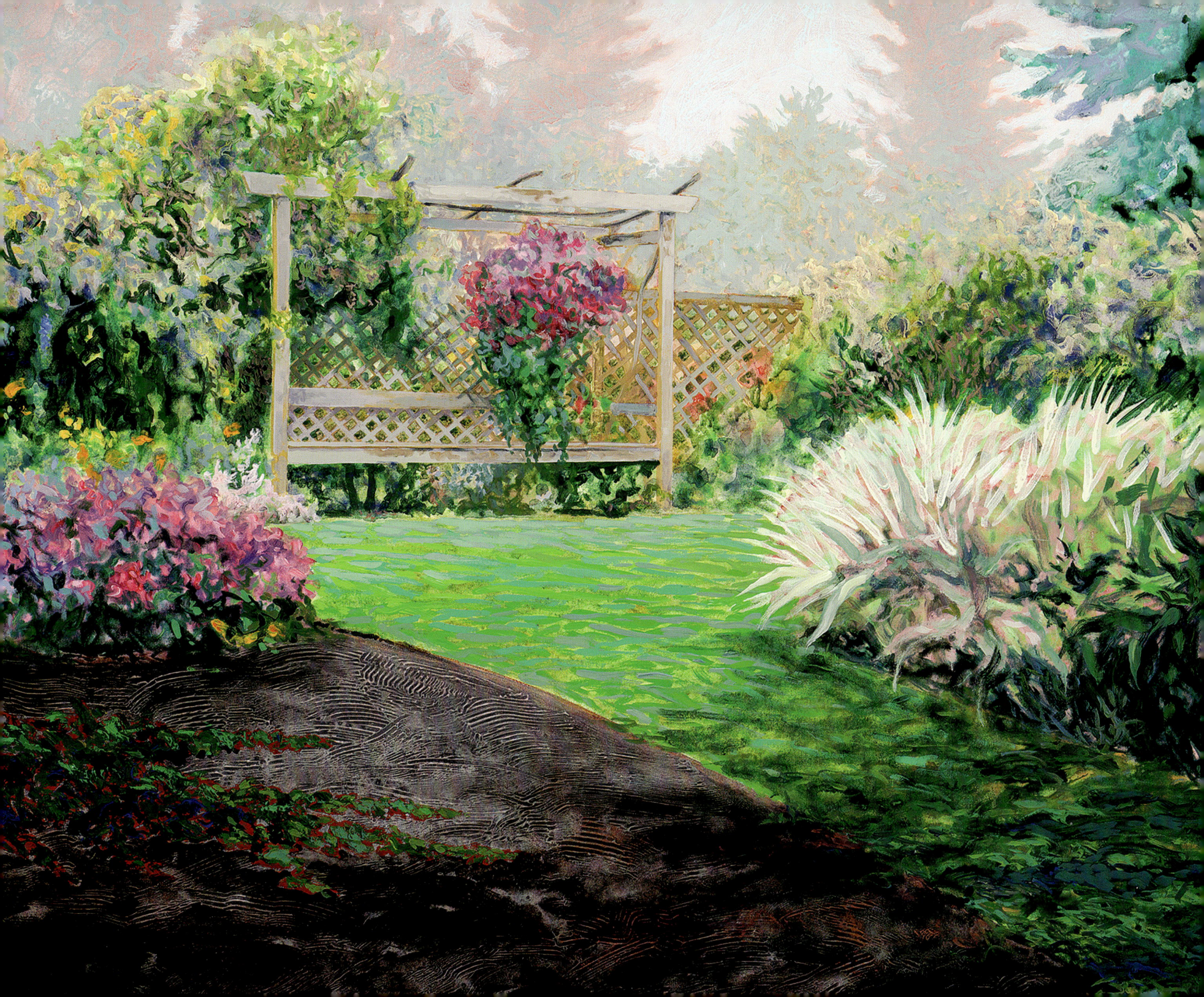

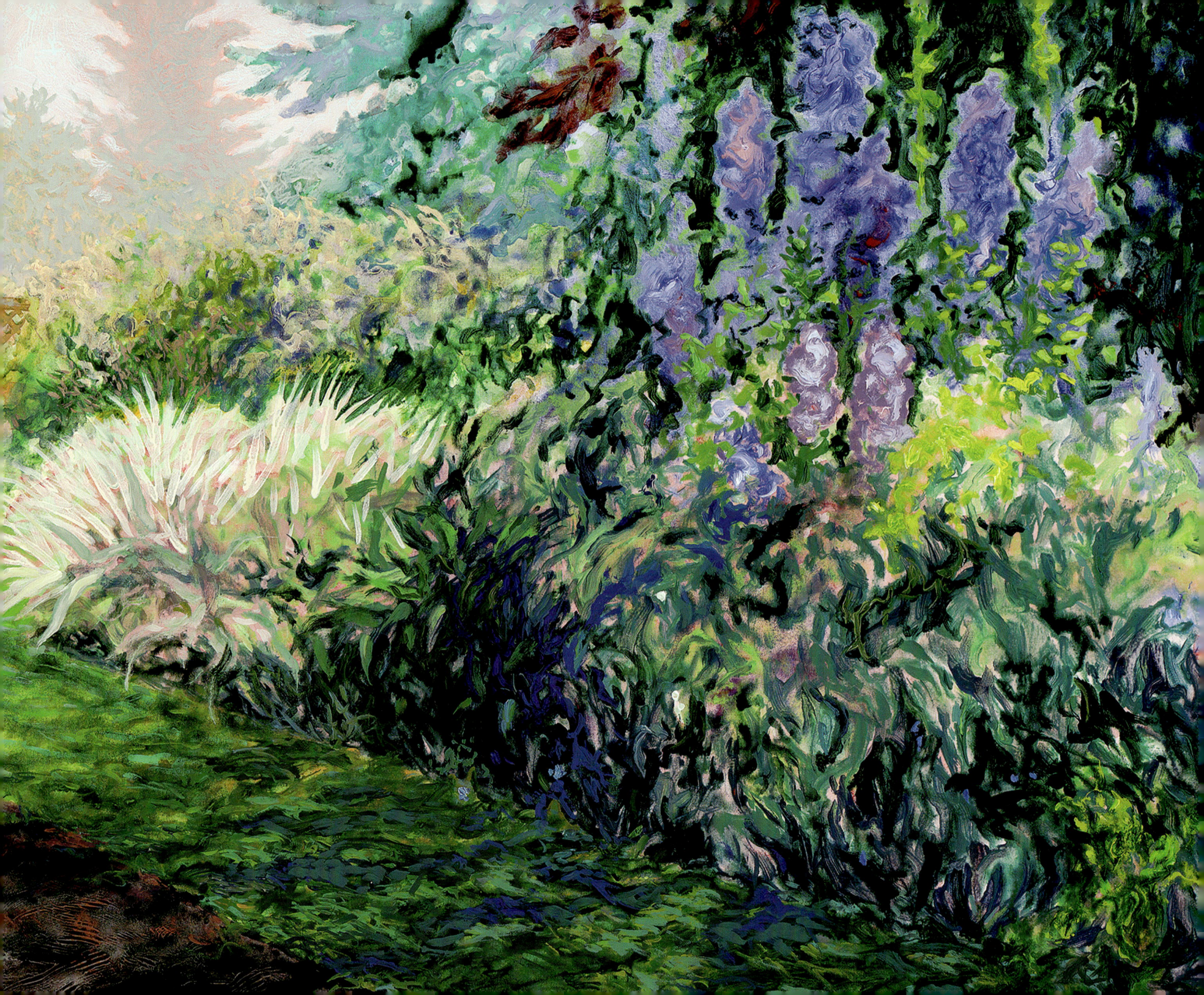

# BENHAVEN GARDEN

Depictions of Benhaven, the Gaelic-inspired name of Yvette and David's garden where they live in Benalto, Alberta, are not the earliest works represented in *Greatest Garden*, but as subject they are a physical and philosophical anchor. Coaxed from the earth, as any garden in Alberta needs to be, the glory of Benhaven takes on many dimensions in colour, plant species, and seasons. Noticeably, too, the old Presbyterian church where Dave and Yvette work, the nearby home where they live, and the all-important garden shed take a back seat in this bucolic setting–sheltering the garden's growth from inclement weather including hail, drought, blizzard, and tornado.

Dating back to 1994 with the purchase of the property in the small hamlet, nearly thirty years of gardening has gone into its realisation. It is a job shared by both artists but overseen by Yvette, where such perennials as gladioli, iris, day lilies, oriental poppies, delphiniums, Maltese crosses, sunflowers, dianthus, and others compete for attention. Favourite prairie annuals such as geraniums and begonias get planted, too, in a mature setting of Japanese maple, lilac hedges, dogwoods, spruce, Russian Maackia, mountain ash, chokecherry, and a Virginia Creeper brought from England in the 1920s.

All the growth which More renders as oil paint on hardboard are *plein-air* evocations, the only exception being the large studio work *Morning Mist at Benhaven*, which, as an acrylic on canvas, provides a wider view of the garden in all its glory–well, a *portion* of its glory, given Benhaven occupies a good swath of the half-acre property. Plein-air (literally: fresh air) is not just creating a sketch on site; it is painting an entire work outdoors. A technique beautifully honed by Tom Thomson and The Group of Seven in their pursuit of wilderness, it was given its shape and definition by the French Impressionists, who sought to convey a transitory feeling or impression of the everyday, especially as experienced outdoors, whether rural or urban. The Benhaven artist, though, more so than the above, accomplishes this with heavier, even lush, applications of paint that can swirl with movement. Nothing seems tame about this garden as it presses forward into our space and consciousness.

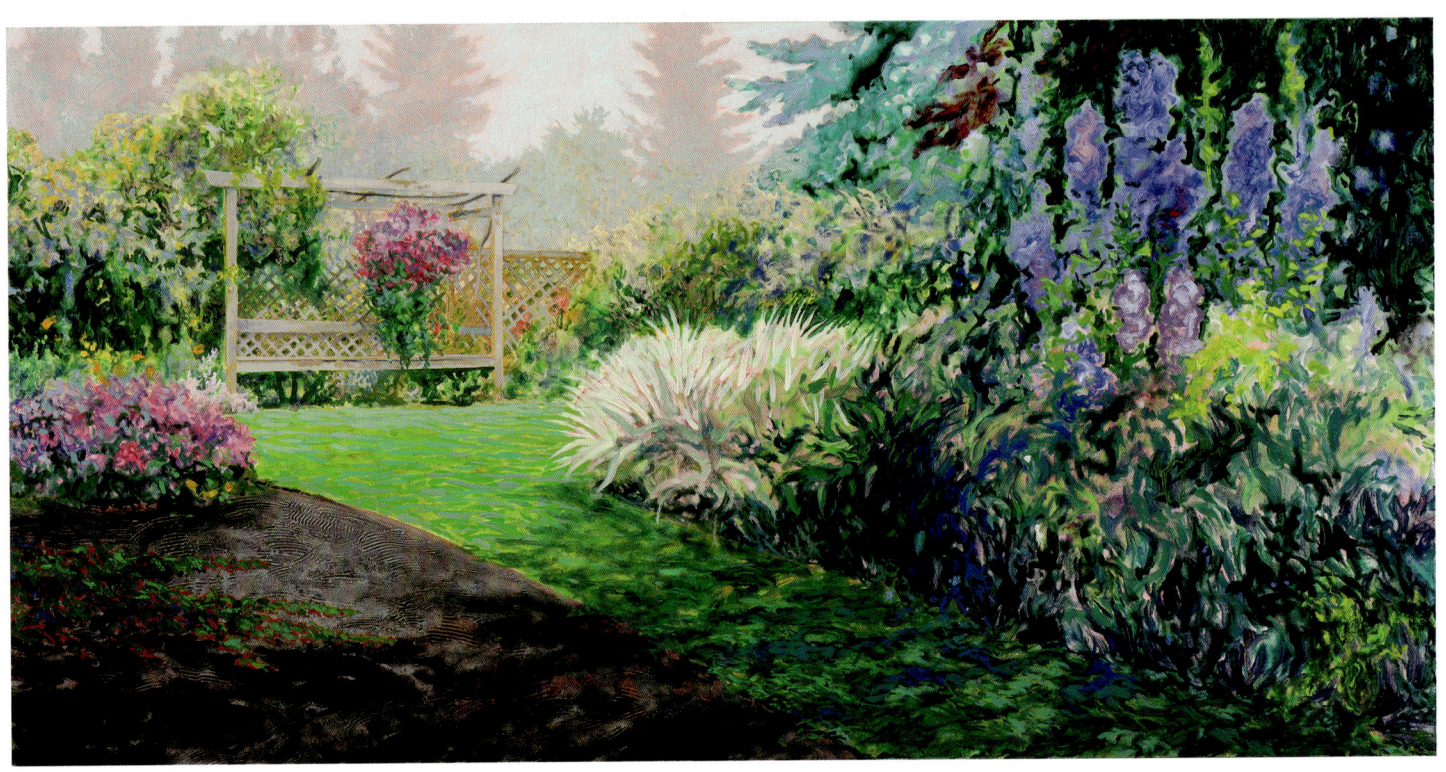

*Morning Mist at Benhaven*, 2007
acrylic on canvas
32 x 72 inches (81.28 x 182.88 cm)
Details of *Morning Mist at Benhaven,* 2007 on pages 11 & 12.

*"The garden invites meandering. There are so many pathways to explore at any time of the year, but summer's cloak makes for hidden treasures that reveal at each turn and step. If I could paint every moment that has astonished me I would need ten lifetimes and endless canvases."*

DAVID MORE (Studio Notes)[1]

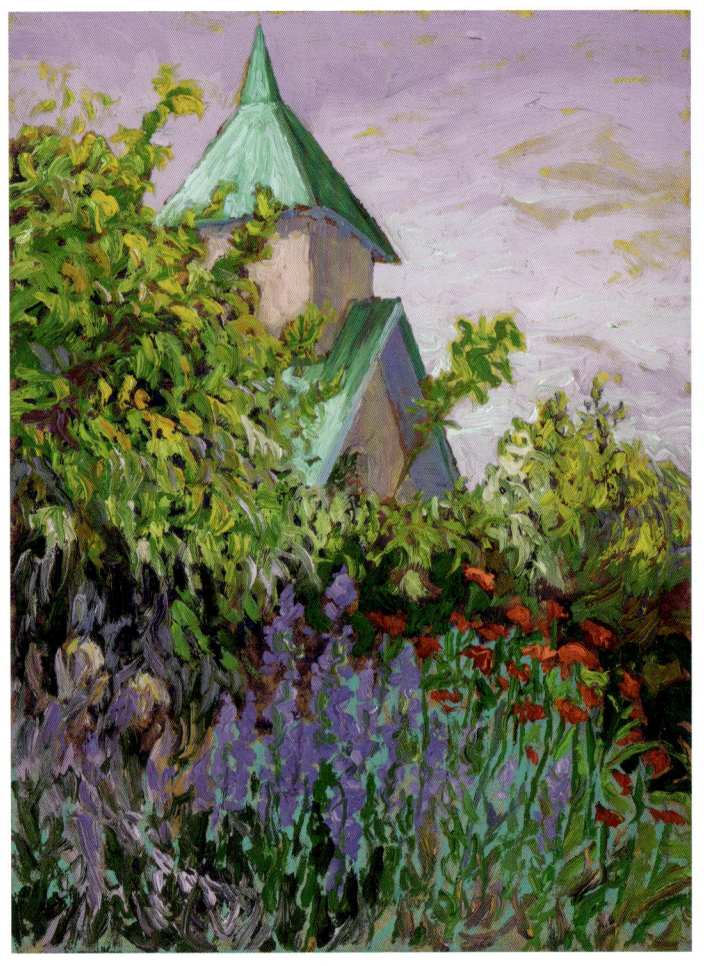

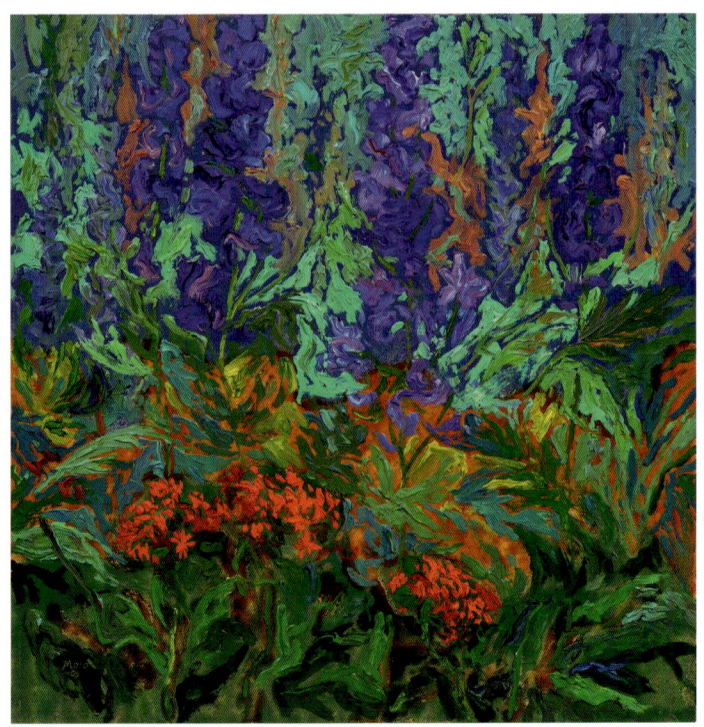

*Morning Heat and Steeple*, 2003
oil on hardboard
16 x 12 inches (40.64 x 30.48 cm)

*Homage to a Zig Zag (Delphiniums & Maltese, July 24)*, 2006
oil on hardboard
16 x 16 inches (40.64 x 40.64 cm)

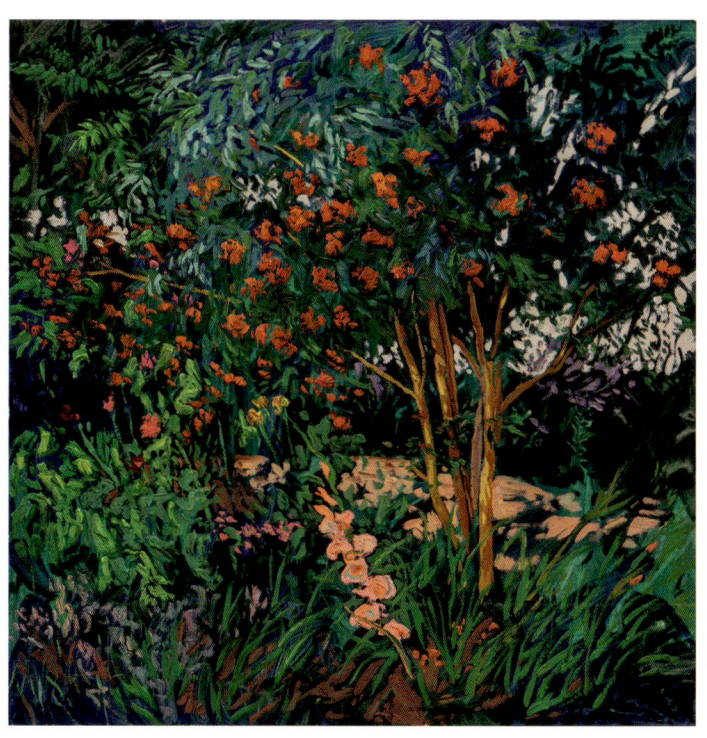

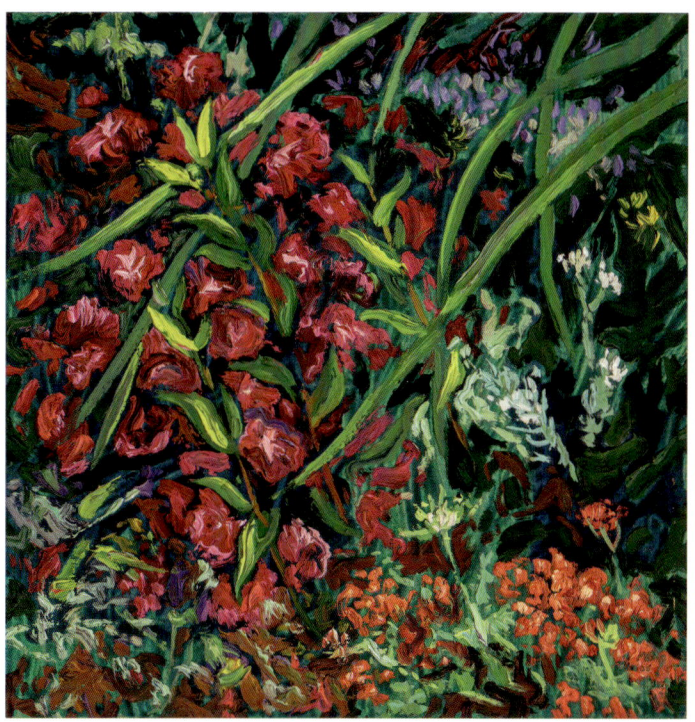

*Mountain Ash Over Gladiolas*, 2005
oil on hardboard
24 x 24 inches (60.96 x 60.96 cm)

*Velvet Red Dianthus*, 2006
oil on hardboard
12 x 12 inches (30.48 x 30.48 cm)

*Garden Portal*, 2008
oil on hardboard
12 x 12 inches (30.48 x 30.48 cm)

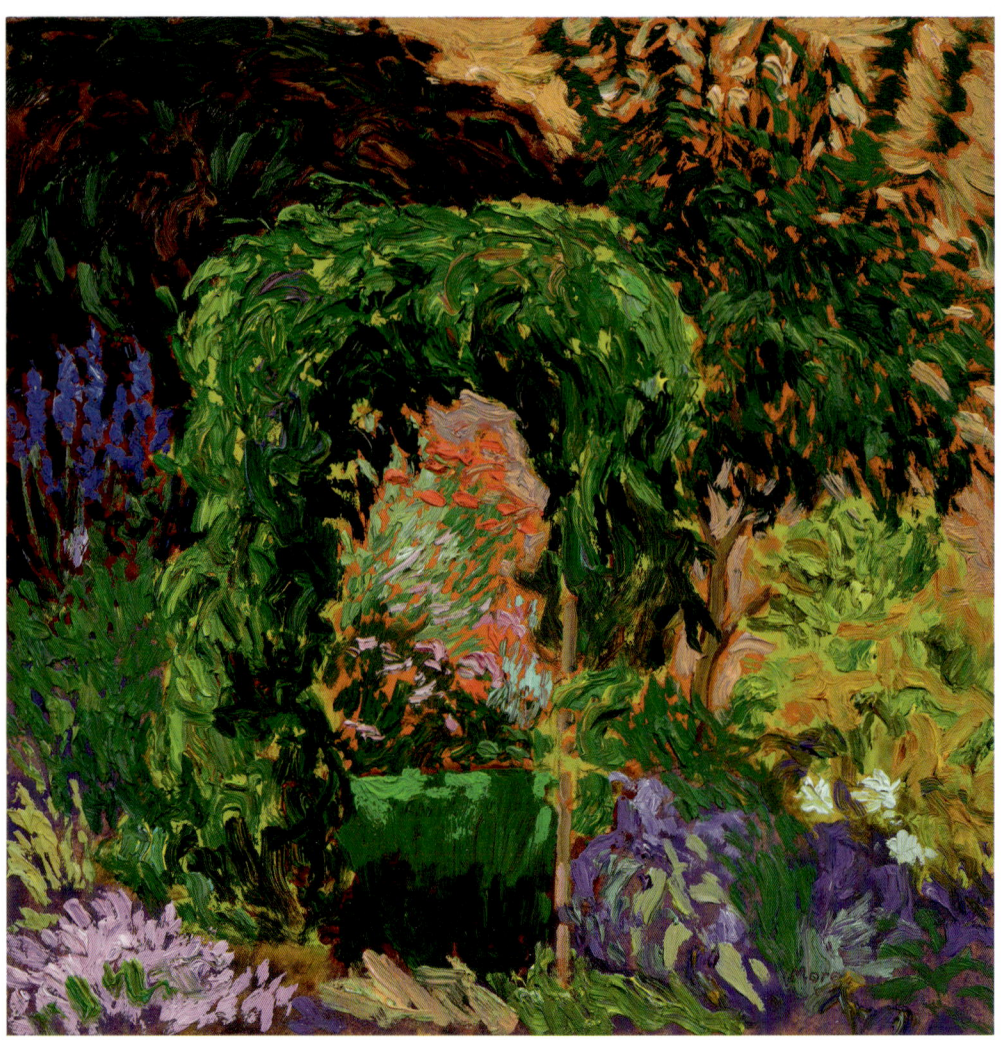

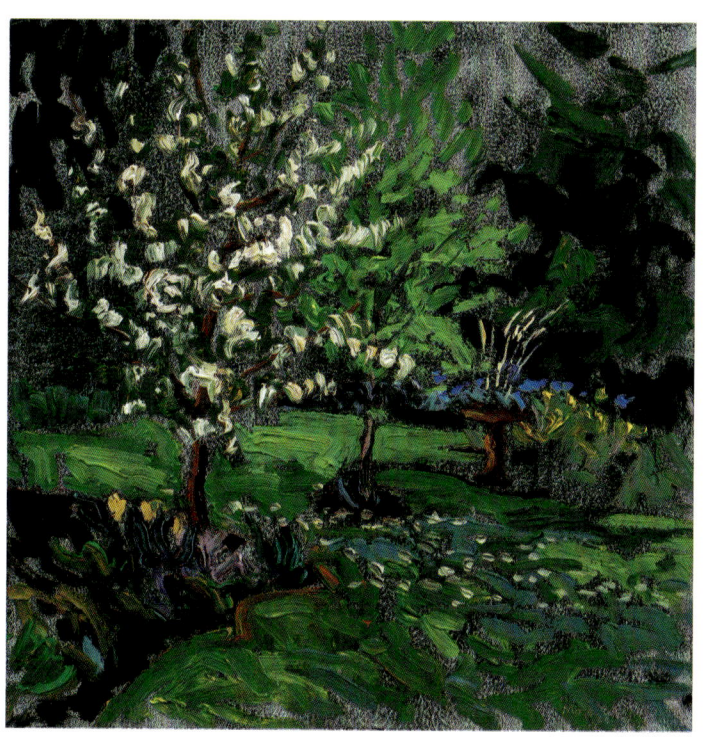

*Petals in the Shadow – Approaching Storm*, 2004
oil on hardboard
12 x 12 inches (30.48 x 30.48 cm)

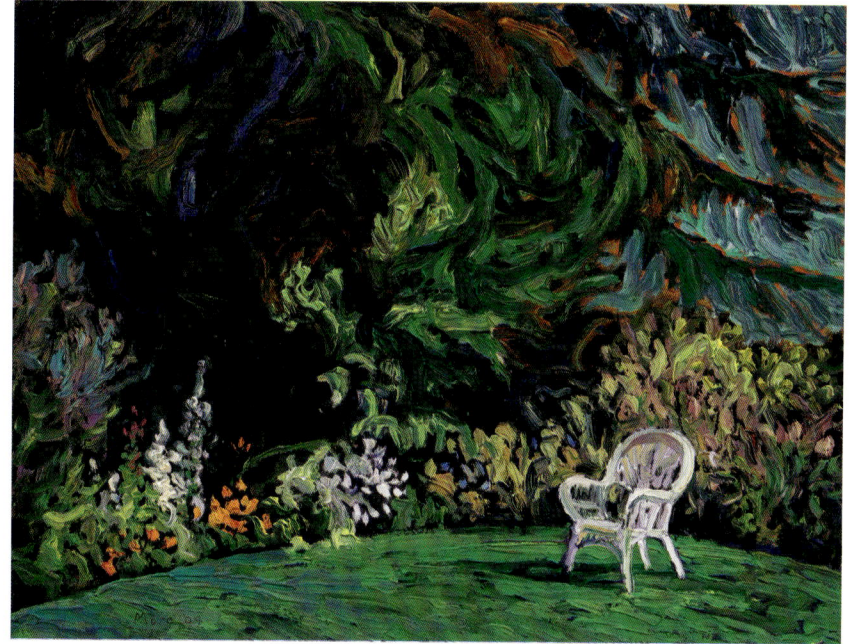

*Chair before Shadows*, 2004
oil on hardboard
12 x 12 inches (30.48 x 30.48 cm)

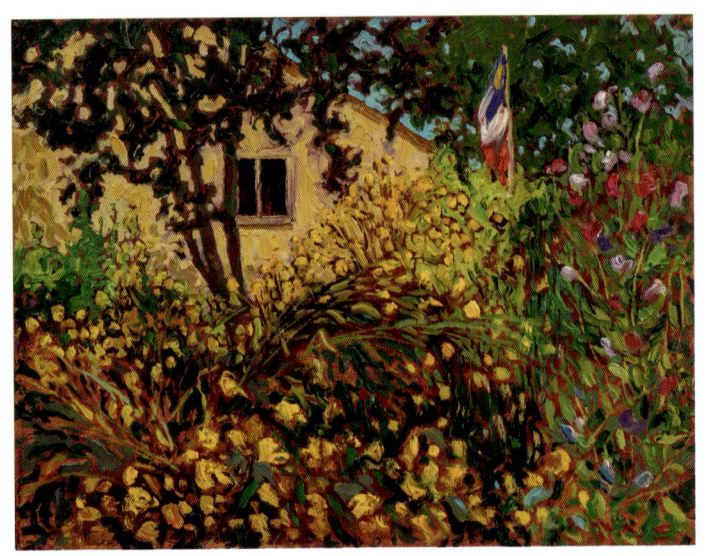

*Sunflowers Bow to September*, 2015
oil on hardboard
12 x 16 inches (30.48 x 40.64 cm)

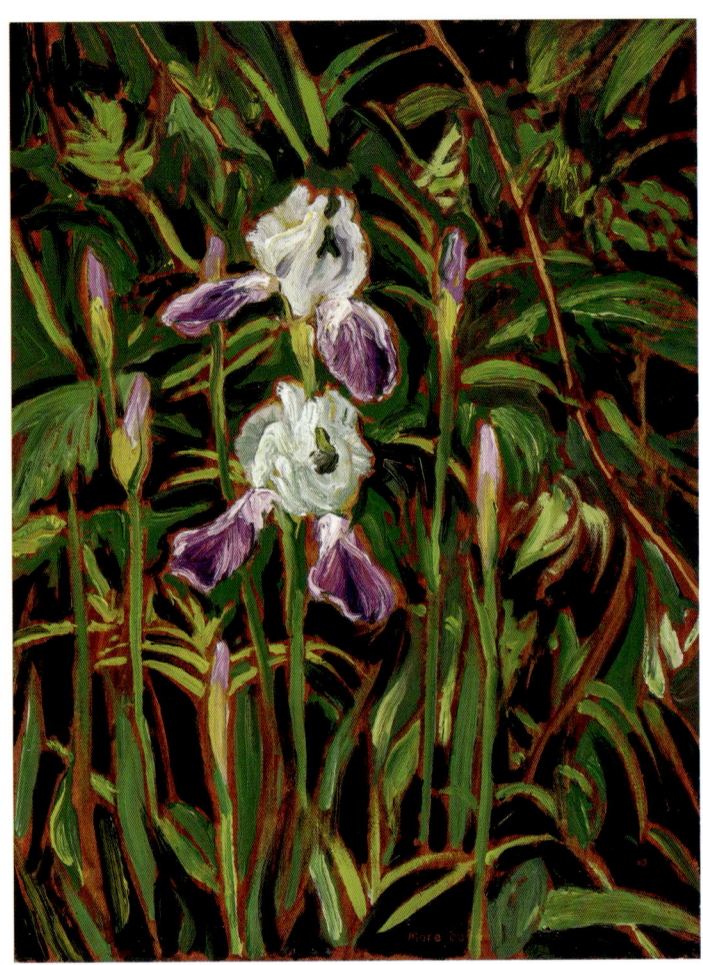

*Tandem Iris*, 2008
oil on hardboard
16 x 12 inches (40.64 x 30.48 cm)

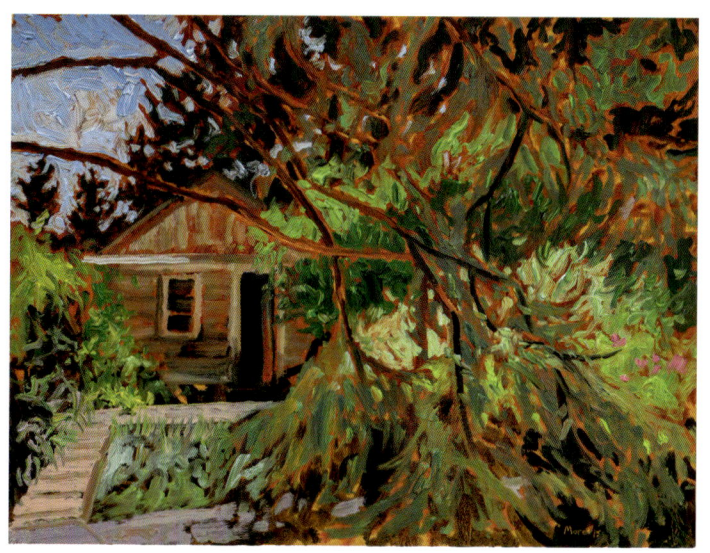

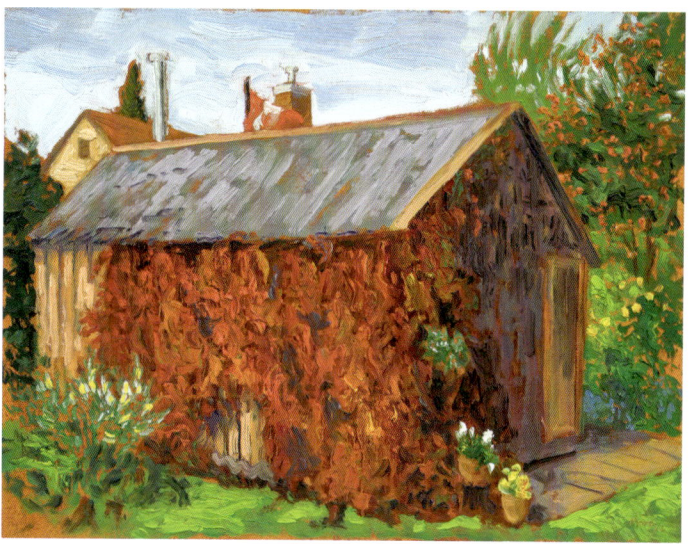

*Sultry Day Beneath Boughs*, 2015
oil on hardboard
12 x 16 inches (30.48 x 40.64 cm)

*Shed in Scarlet*, 2015
oil on hardboard
12 x 16 inches (30.48 x 40.64 cm)

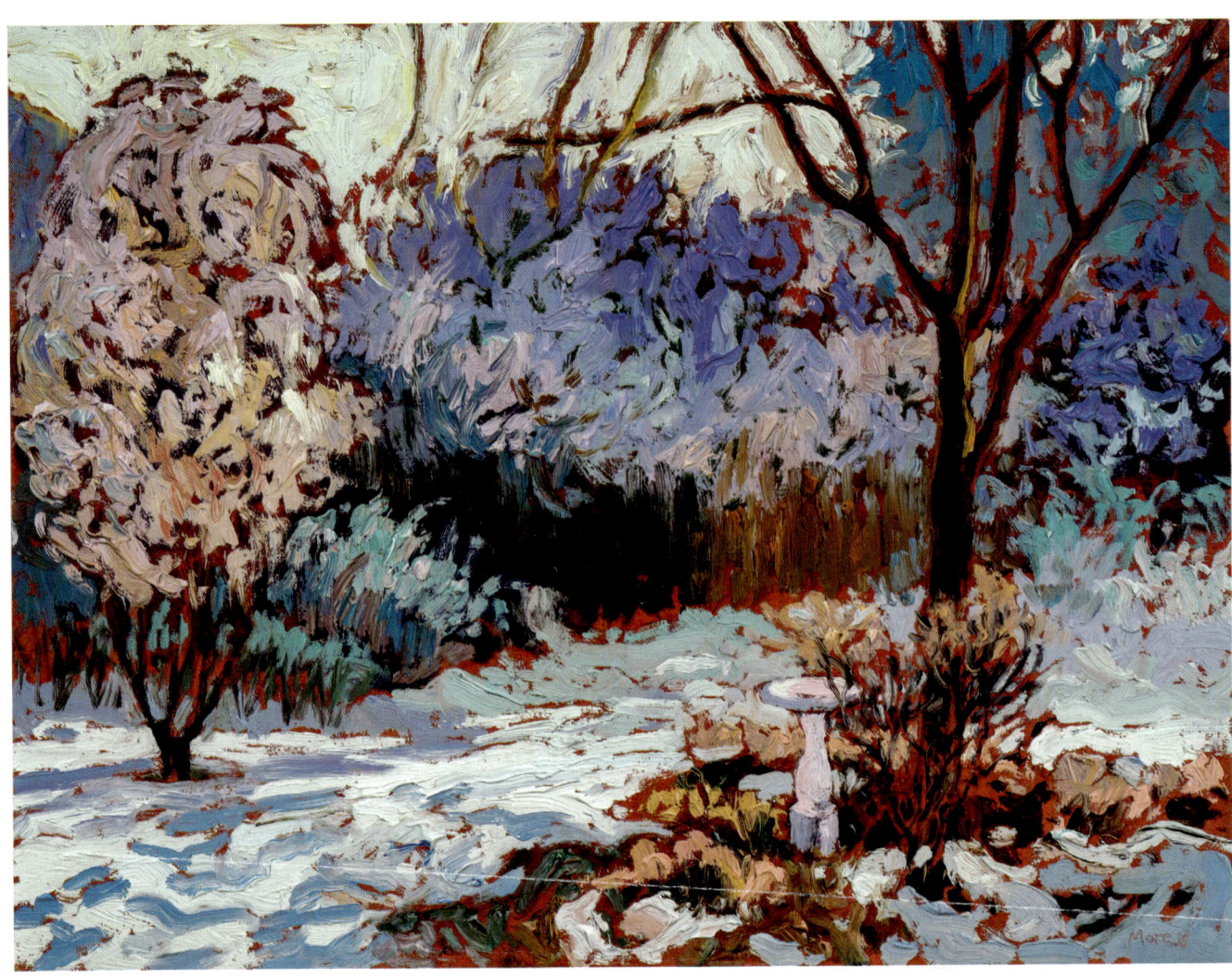

*Winter's Bath, January 30*, 2015
oil on hardboard
12 x 16 inches (30.48 x 40.64 cm)

*"In the process of creating gardens, we expound on who we are: selecting chromas to proclaim our joy at the rebirth of spring, planting the subtle hues to induce meditation, building walkways to lead us, and shaped formal beds to define our edges."*

Davɪᴅ Moʀᴇ (Studio Notes)[2]

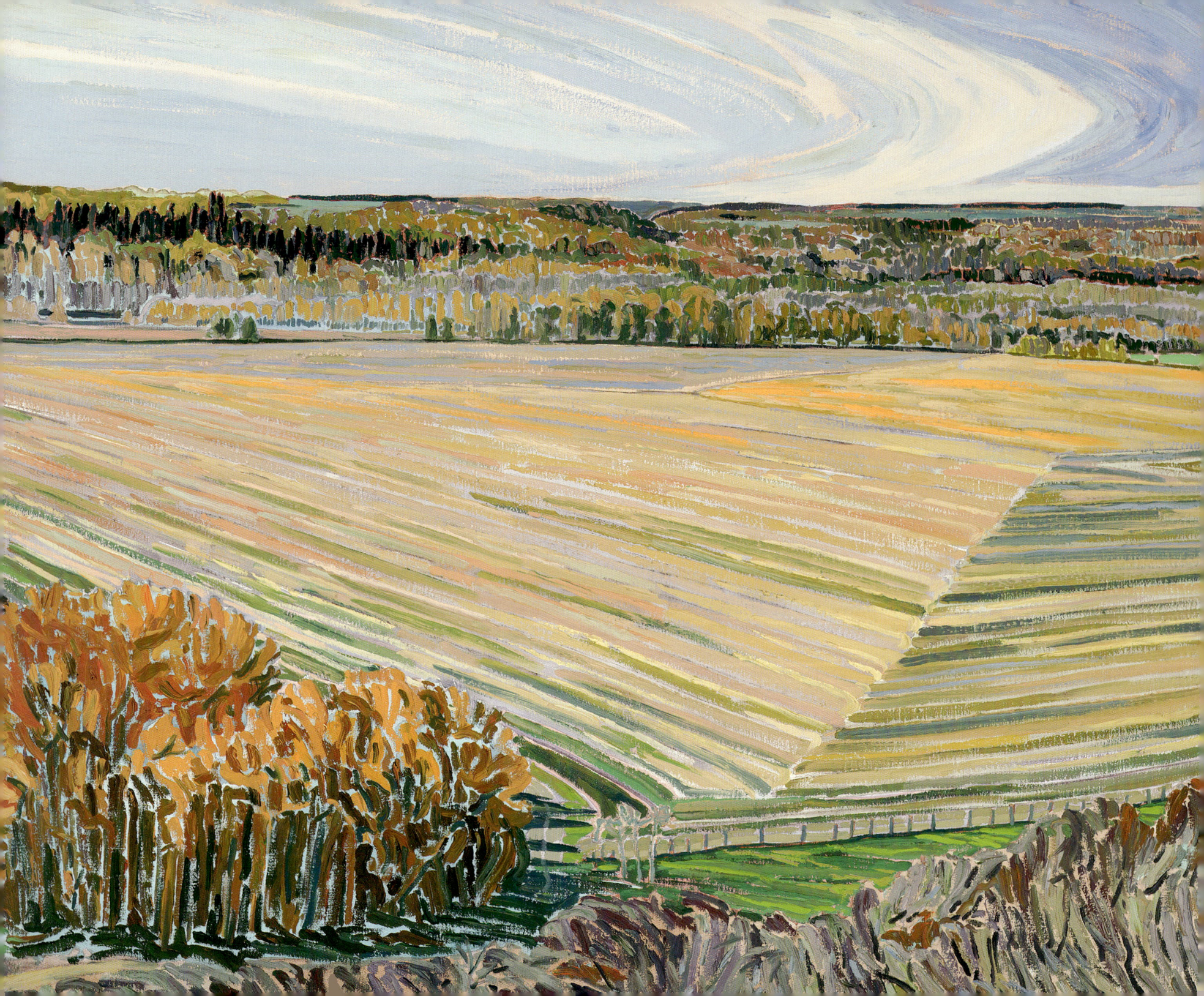

# LOCAL WANDERINGS (NEAR & AFAR)

Wandering is a lifelong enthusiasm for David More. Going to places connected to the idea of the greatest garden that spills out around him, he explores sites Instagram followers would likely overlook, but for the artist have intrinsic worth nonetheless. They are simply places to *be* both artistically and spiritually. There, not so much for their *scenic* value–a strong thread in Canadian landscape painting and on Instagram–but for what they reflect about where the artist has been as an observer.

Many of the artworks in this chapter feature places found near his rural home, such as *Harvest Forms, Red Deer River Valley* (1986). The oil on canvas was painted two years after More returned to his hometown from Vancouver Island. A sizable work at five feet in length, *Harvest Forms*, is about a particular moment in the Fall. There is a sense of gracious regard for the bounty alluded to in the painting.

Farming is a large-scale activity in central Alberta, and the endless linear rows in the field gave the artist an opportunity to work with subtle, complementary hues, ranging from greenish-blue to peachy pinks to yellowish orange. In comparison, the poplar copse in the bottom-left stands to attention in its full autumn colours. Even more striking is the perspective: the field an optical illusion, tilted-upwards, its harvested rows a 'podium' below the curvilinear sky. A rough fringe of greys in the foreground is repeated in the background amidst the poplar and pine. In this clustering of colours, harmony abounds.

In other works represented in the Red Deer & District Museum Society Art Collection, the forest dweller comes alive in two plein-air (oil on hardboard) pictures painted during More's two-year Vancouver Island sojourn. Later came pieces that compelled him to paint the nearby meandering Medicine River and, at twilight, the ominous decaying tangle of forest and ground cover he saw in the Alberta foothills and in New Brunswick.

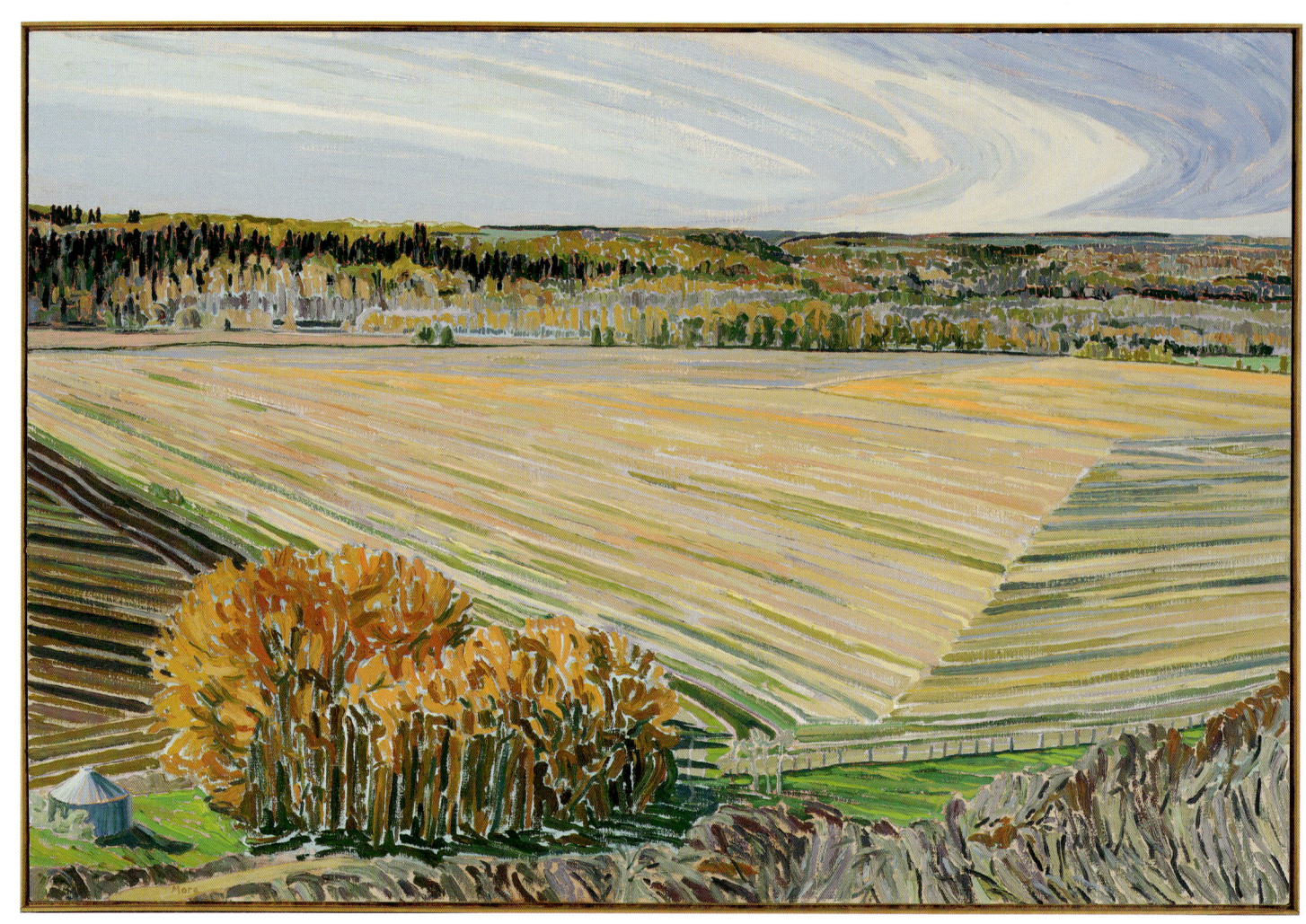

*Harvest Forms, Red Deer River Valley*, 1986
oil on canvas
40 x 60 inches (101.6 x 152.4 cm)
Detail of *Harvest Forms, Red Deer River Valley*, 1986 on page 24.

The Medicine River is one of several small rivers criss-crossing the green belt of central Alberta with its greenhouses and market gardens. Like most waterways, it has not always benefitted from flowing through large swaths of farmland. In this quartet of artworks, the artist is aware the Medicine is more than just a convenient source of water for livestock and other purposes. Also known in Cree as the Sundance River, its meaning derived from the words *musk-iki* and *nipagwasimow*, the river was also the setting for a Thomas King novel and film titled *Medicine River*.

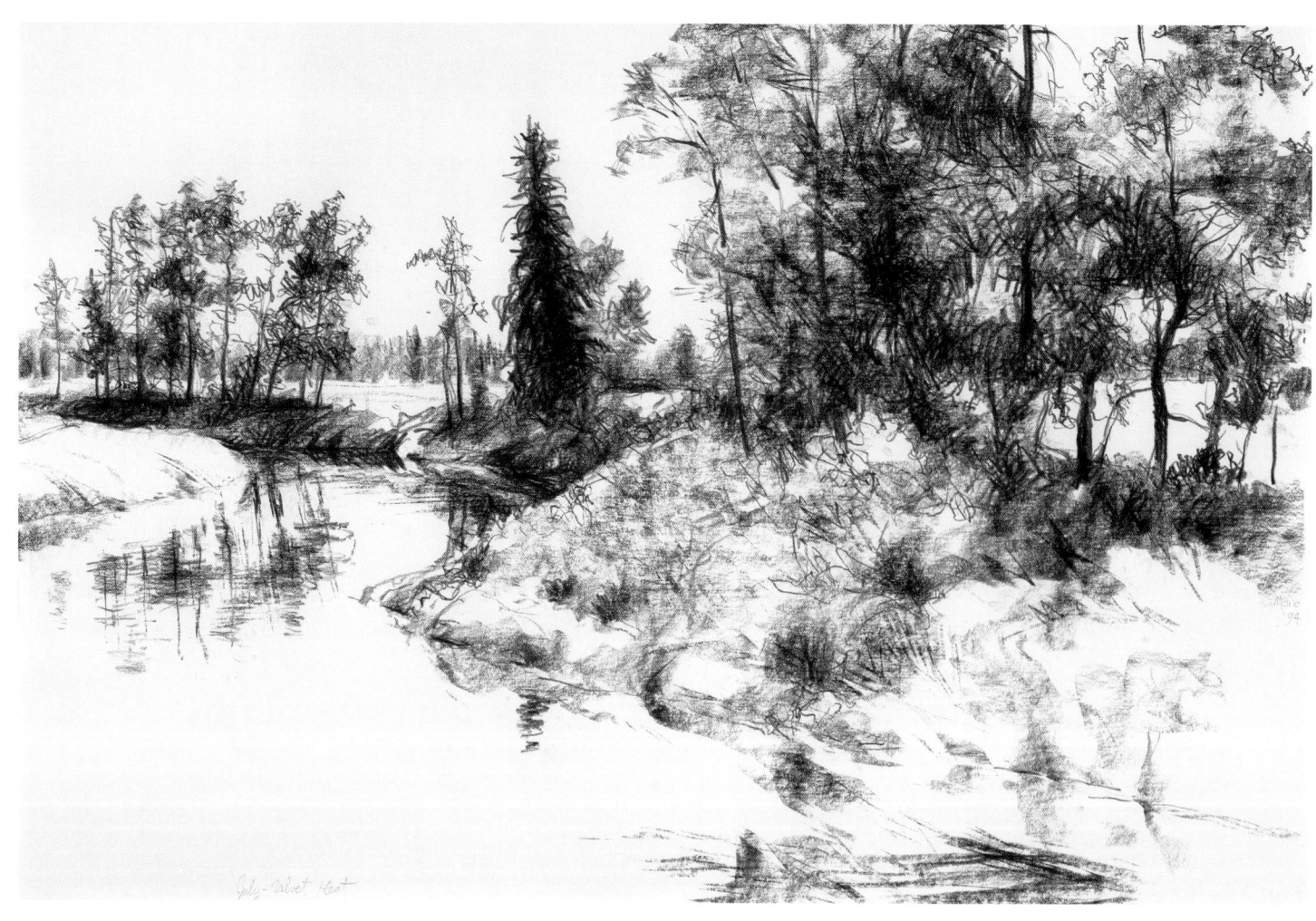

*Study for July Velvet Heat (Medicine River)*, 1995
black conte on paper
15.5 x 23.75 inches (39.37 x 60.325 cm)

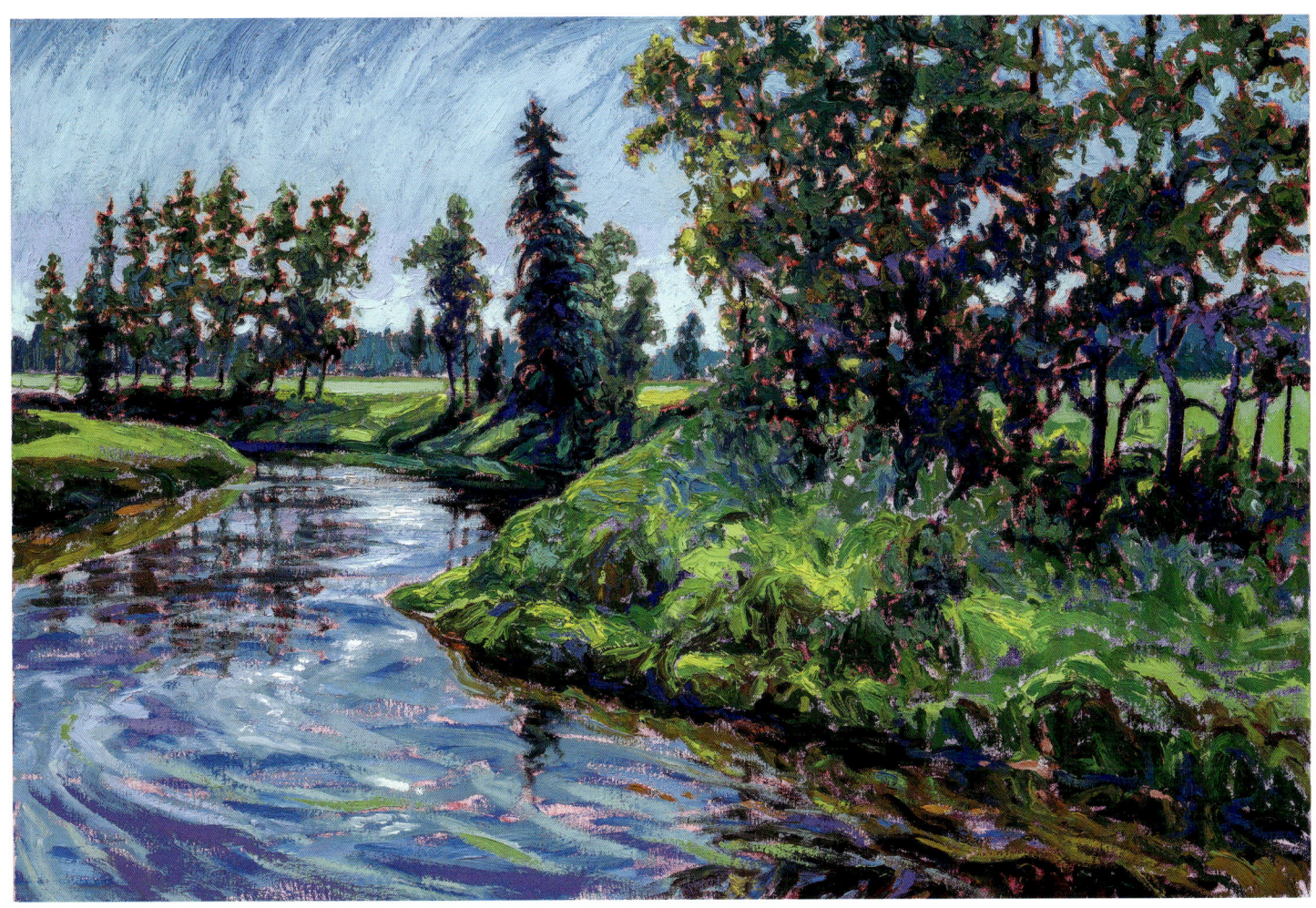

*July Velvet Heat (Medicine River)*, 1995
oil on canvas
20 x 30 inches (50.8 x 76.2 cm)

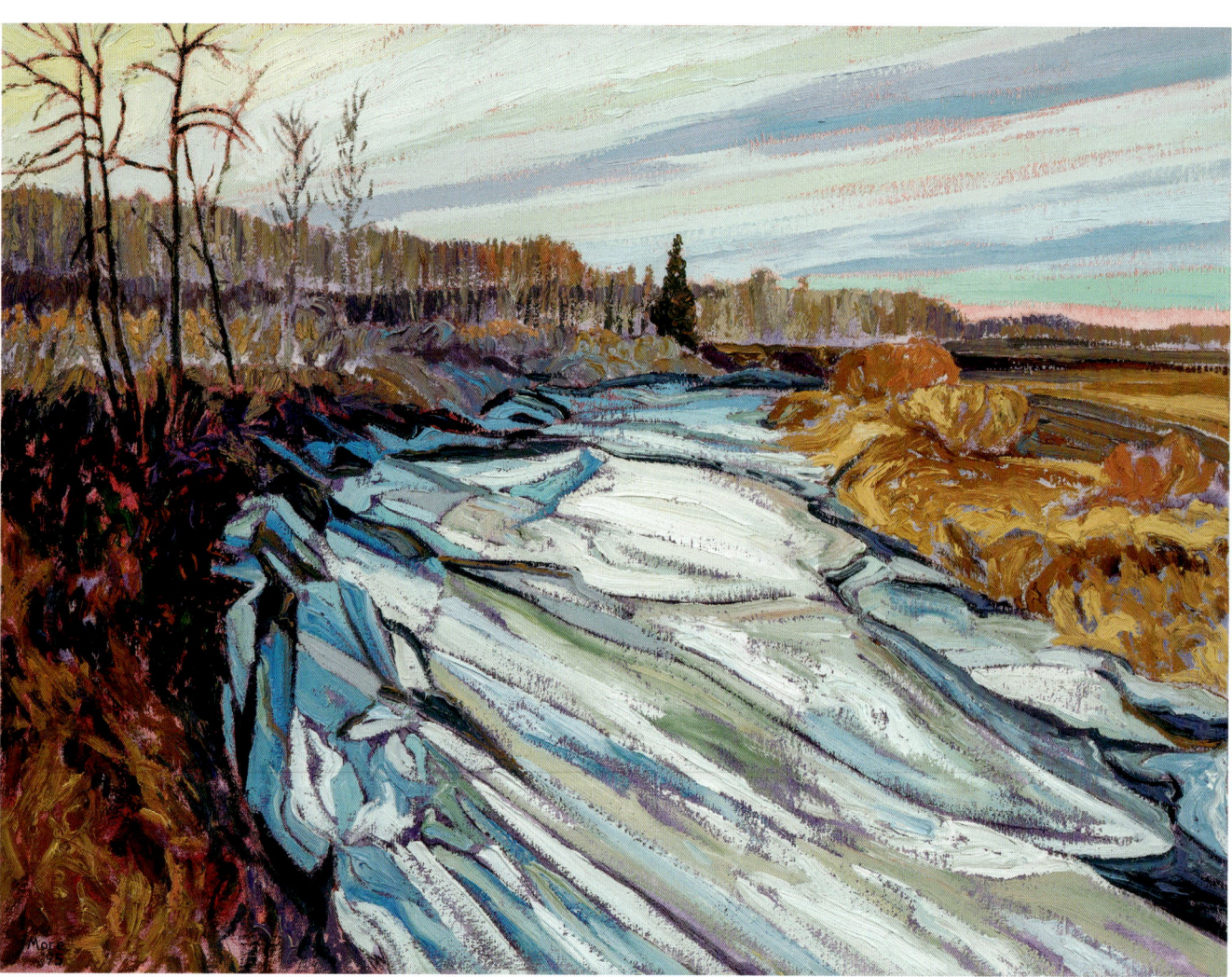

*Spring Ice Forms Along the Medicine*, 1995
oil on canvas
24 x 32 inches (60.96 x 81.28 cm)

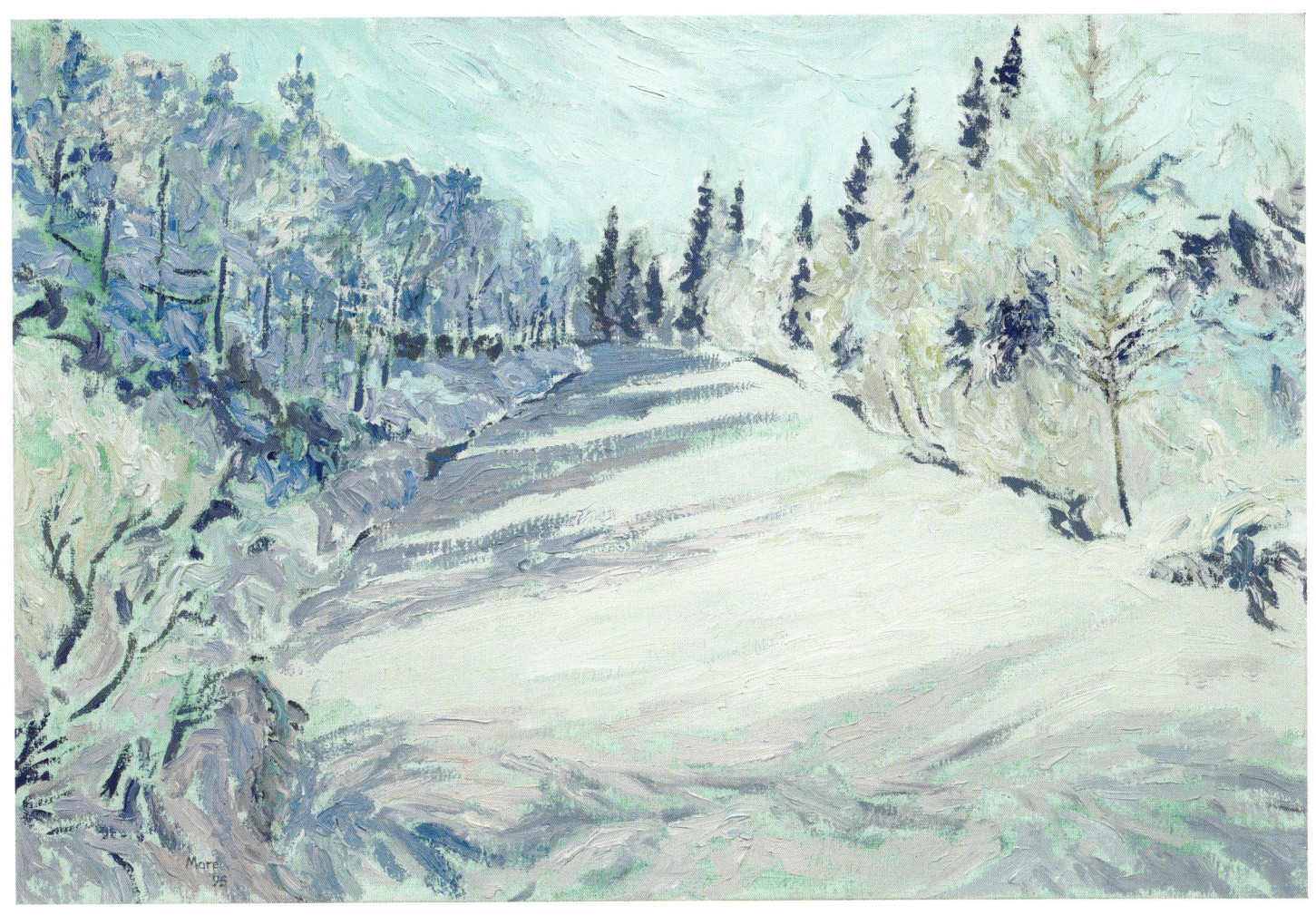

*Winter Afternoon Along the Medicine*, 1995
oil on canvas
20 x 30 inches (50.8 x 76.2 cm)

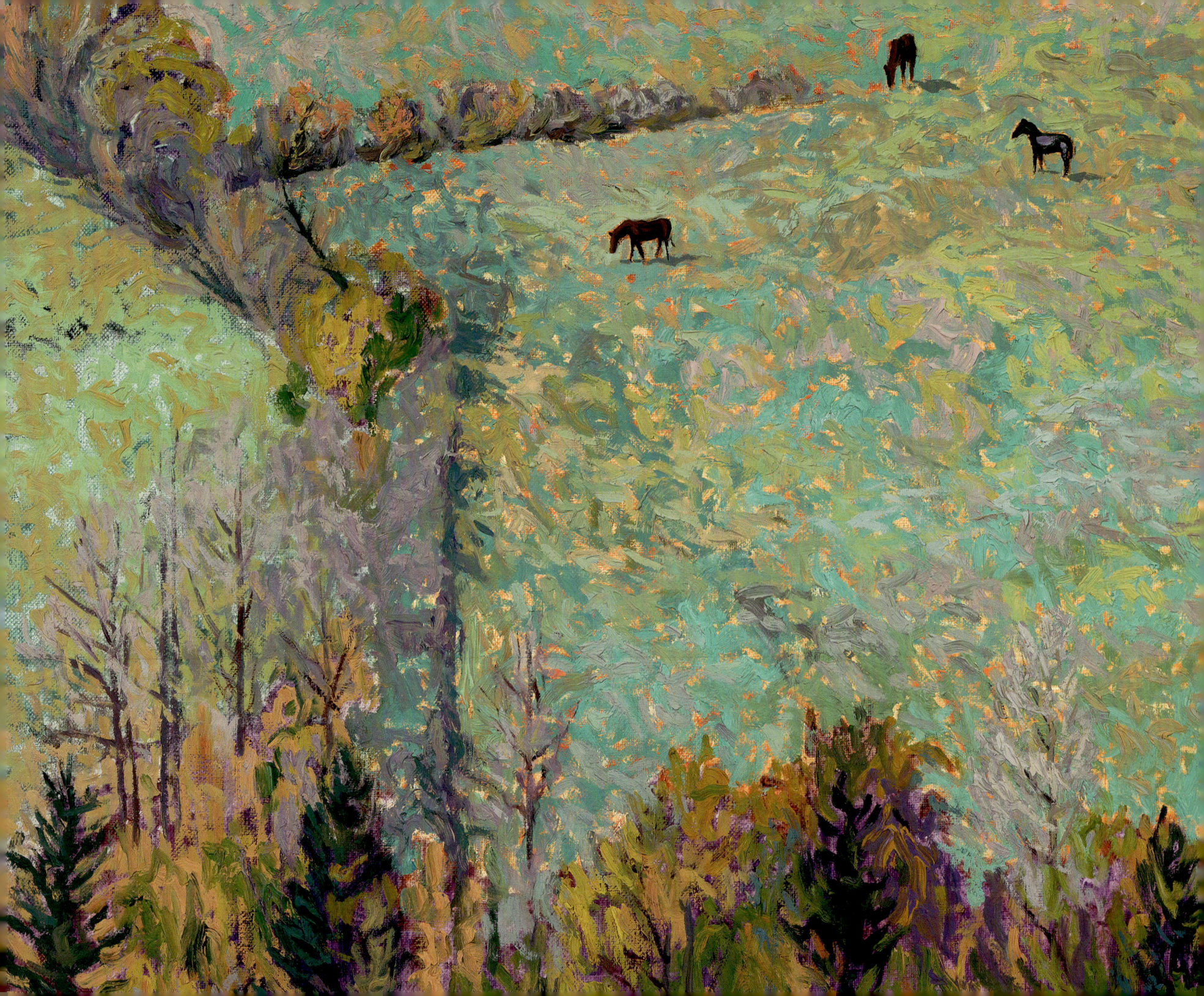

*"As a painter, memory plays a huge role. A landscape sketch often begins with an initial reaction that tells me: 'This is a great scene. Look at the light…' No sooner have I done a quick pencil sketch…and the light and shadow have gone or shifted. At this point I must be driven by the initial memory, with my study as a guide."*

DAVE MORE (Studio Notes)[1]

*Horses Above the River*, 1995
oil on linen
30 x 30 inches (76.2 x 76.2 cm)
Detail of *Horses Above the River*, 1995 on
page 32.

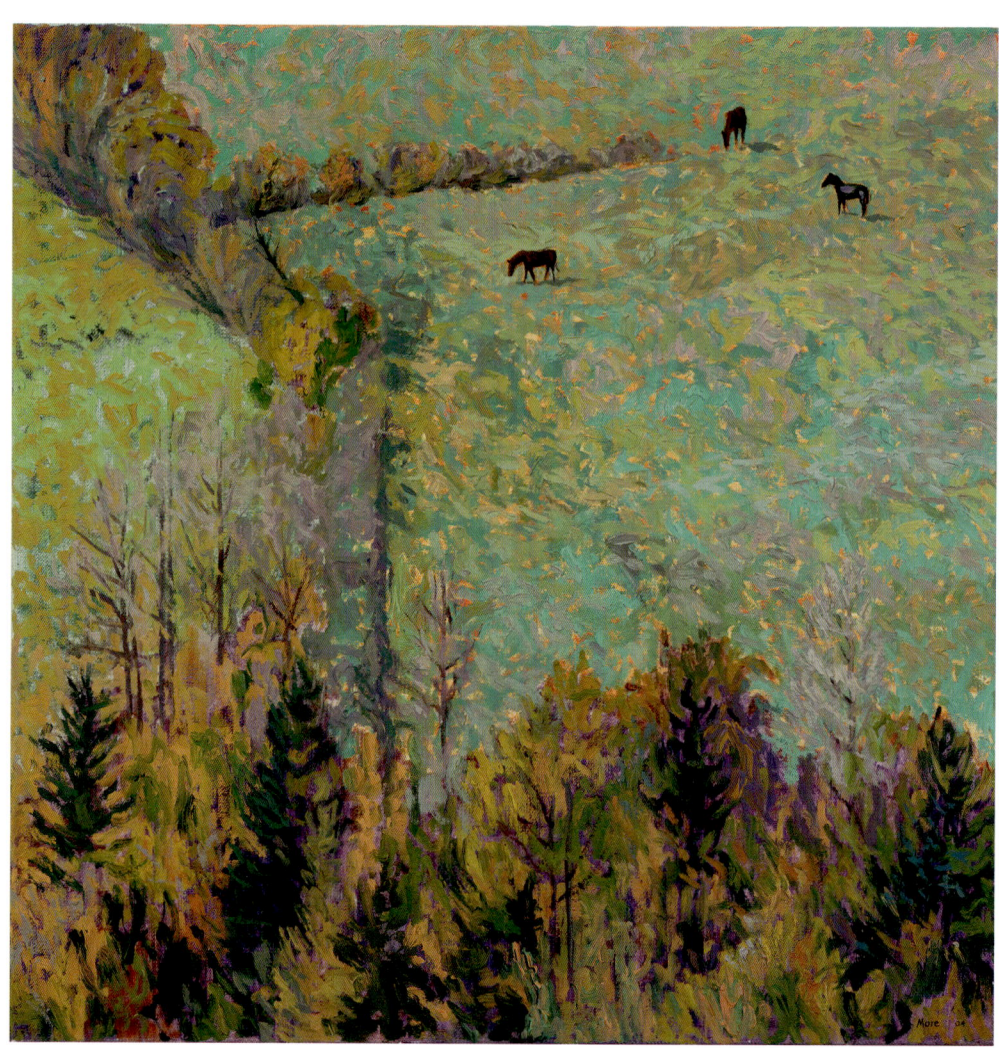

Yes, look at the light, but more importantly look at the daring palette of colours revealed in *Horses Above the River*. Painted on linen, the pasture is pure memory where on a peach/pink ground a beautiful layering of turquoise blue, mauve, and some green turn this familiar Alberta scene into a lyrical treatment. Remove the horses and the painting becomes all the more abstract, a play on expressive brushwork which gives not just form but also a lively impressionistic sparkle to a special time and place.

*Forest Edge by Morning* (Vancouver Island), 1983
oil on hardboard
24 x 24 inches (60.96 x 60.96 cm)

Detail of *Forest Edge by Morning* (Vancouver Island), 1983 on page 38.

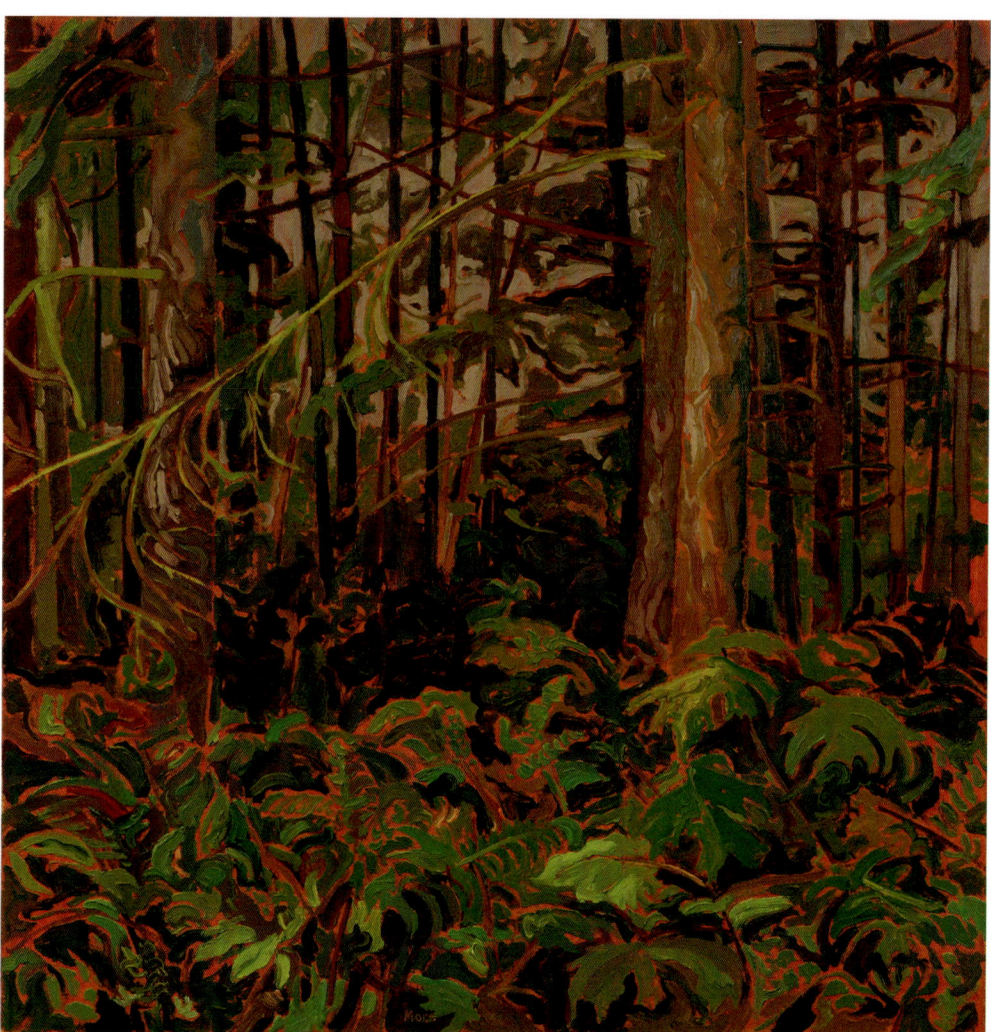

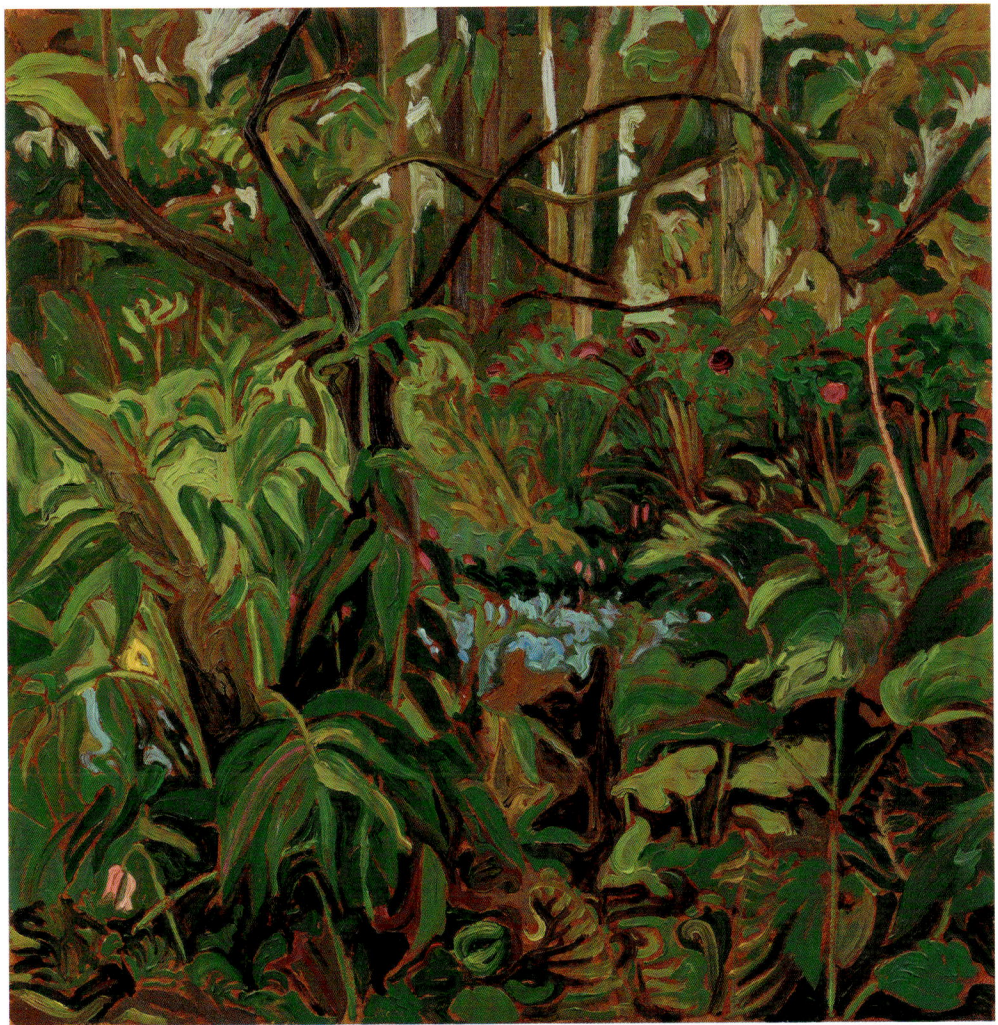

*Forest Passage beneath the Salmonberries*
(Vancouver Island), 1983
oil on hardboard
24 x 24 inches (60.96 x 60.96 cm)

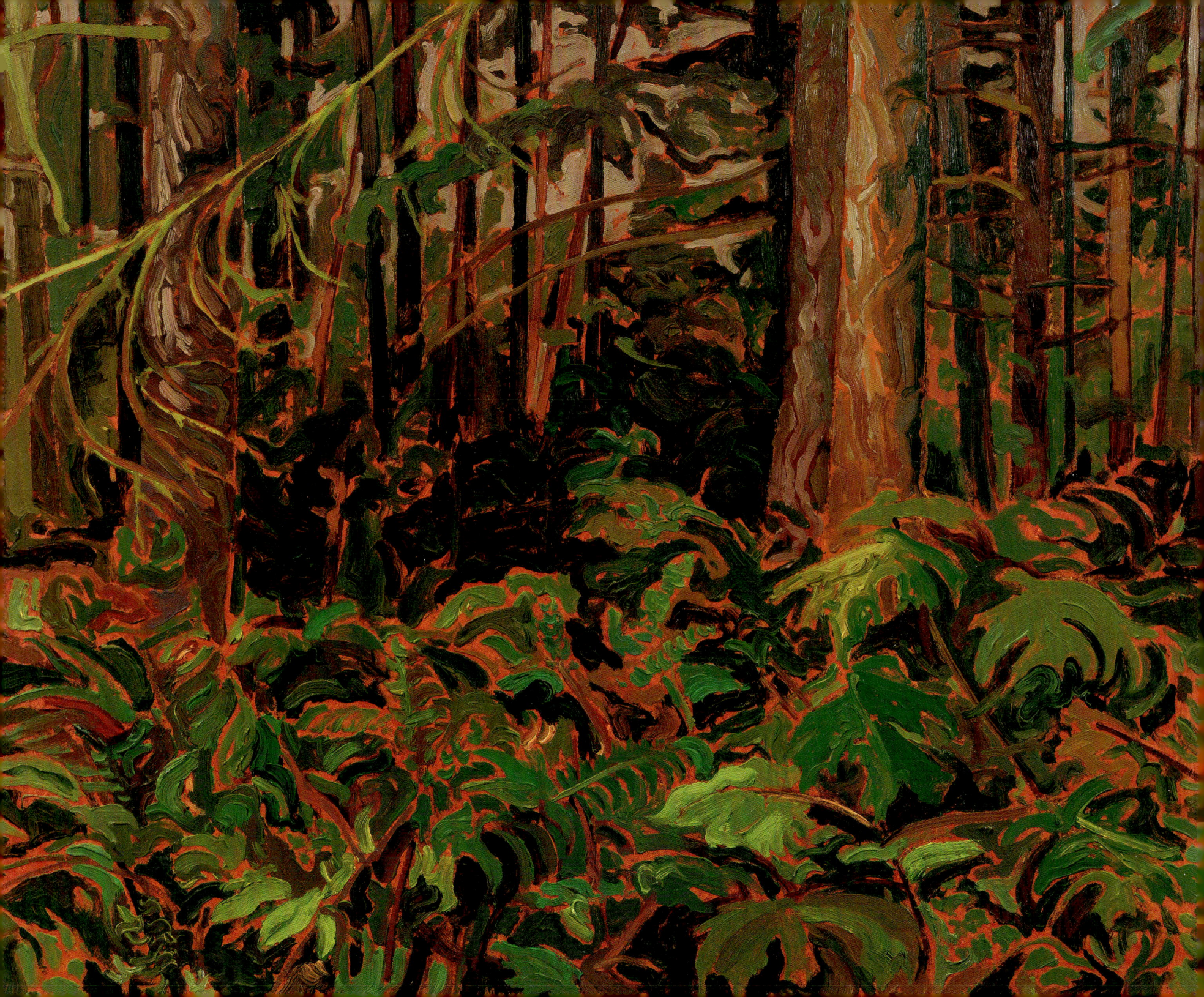

*"Filled with a sense of movement, these twilight images are a metaphor for nature's ambiguity. The paint is knifed on in arm-loads, creating slashing impressionistic surfaces. Indistinct forms appear as through a fog, often creating a feeling of vertigo. David More reaches through the twilight forests."*

CHARLES MEGGISON (*David More: infusion/forest*)[2]

Red Deer area artist Charles Meggison refers to David More as a forest dweller,[3] and certainly many of the terrains he has absorbed–in Vancouver Island, the Red Deer region, and northern New Brunswick–are just that. In *Infusion–Ravine Rising to Light*, the breaking daylight spills forth as oil on canvas. Created over twenty years ago under the theme of *infusion/forest*, the other light-focused works are about twilight, which, in themselves, added another dimension to the series.

Twilight, that in-between period between darkness and light, represented for the artist a dusky moment in time when human consciousness about climate change and its impact on our forests hovered between awareness and the unmindful. Represented in this selection of works in the Red Deer Museum collection are works in oil on canvas, mixed media on paper, and charcoal on paper. Perspective is again important, our view confined to a low vantage point and a flattened perspective. Infused with shifting light among the skeletal vegetation, on full display is More's aptitude for energetic mark-making and abstracted imagery.

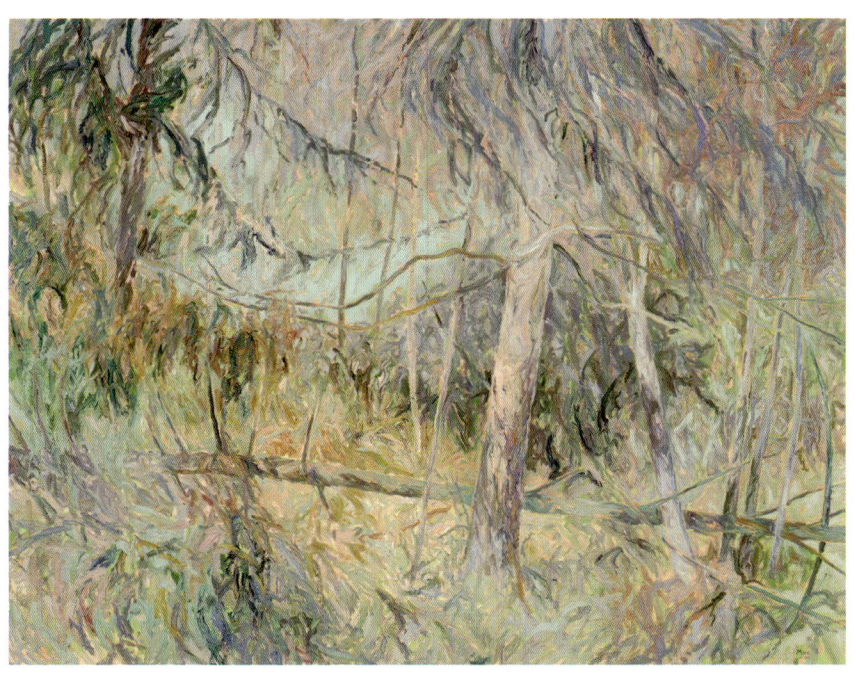

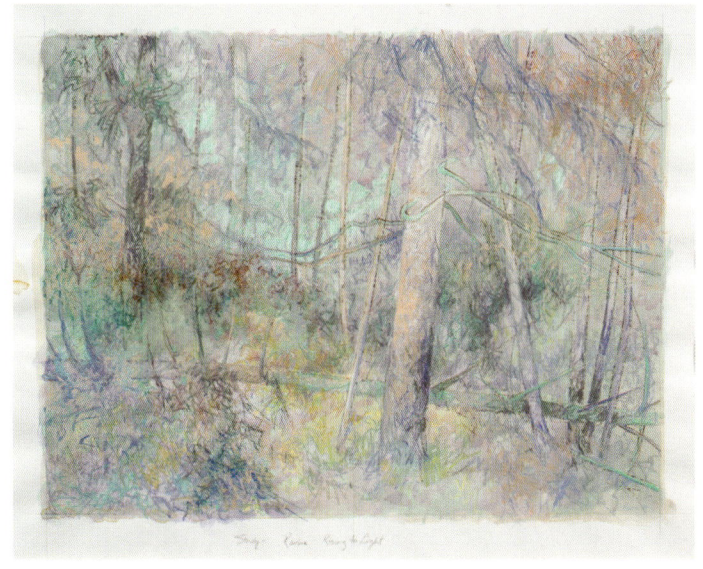

*Infusion – Ravine Rising to Light*, 1999
oil on canvas
60 x 80 inches (152.4 x 152.4 cm)

*Infusion – Ravine Rising to Light* (*Study*), 1999
mixed media on paper
18 x 24 inches (45.72 x 60.96 cm)

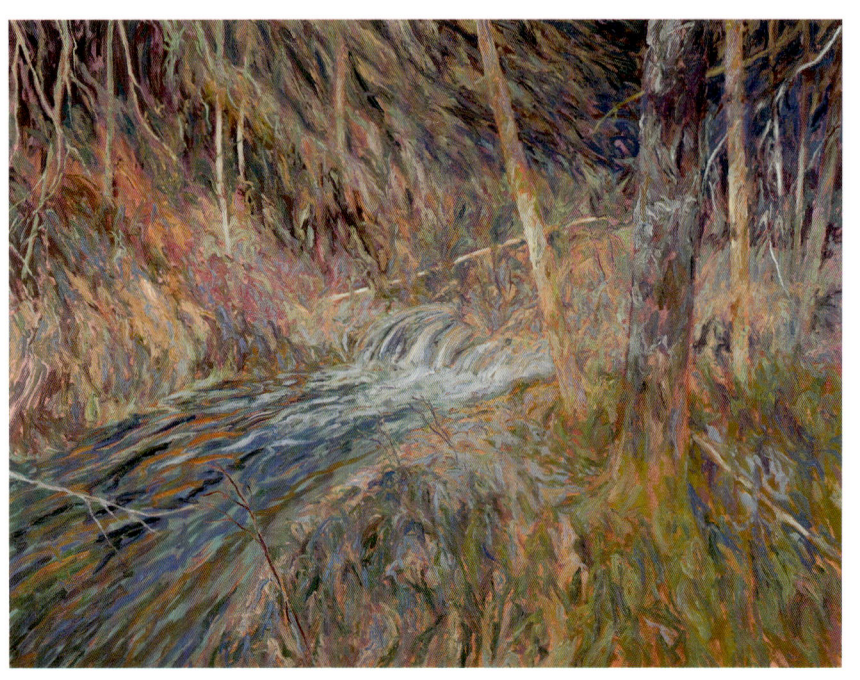

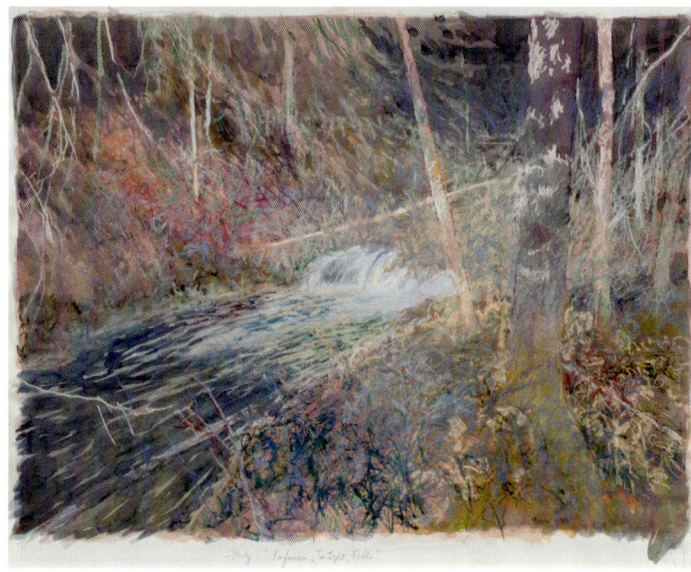

*Infusion – Twilight Falls* (New Brunswick), 1999
oil on canvas
60 x 80 inches (152.4 x 203.2 cm)

*Infusion – Twilight Falls* (*Study*), 1999
mixed media on paper
18 x 24 inches (45.72 x 60.96 cm)

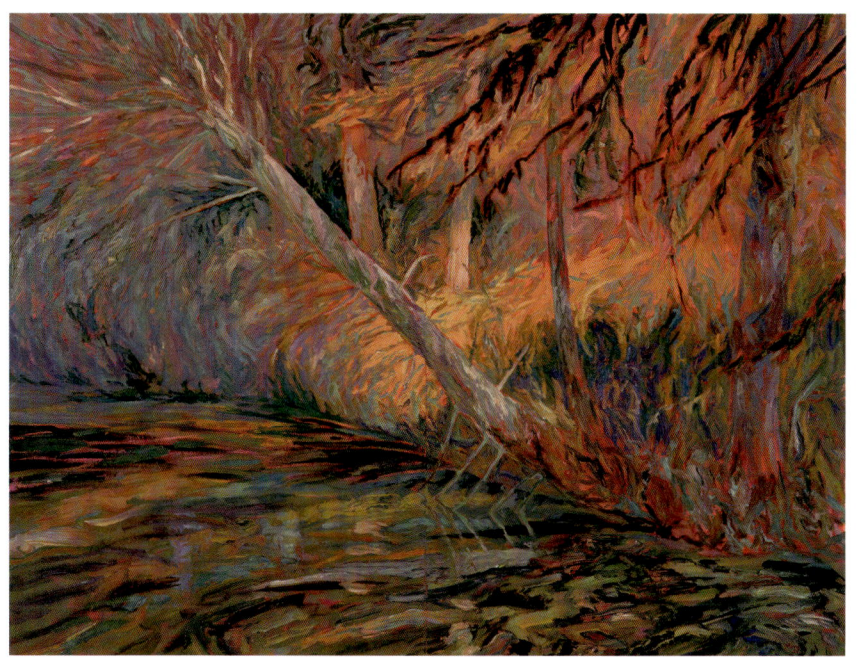

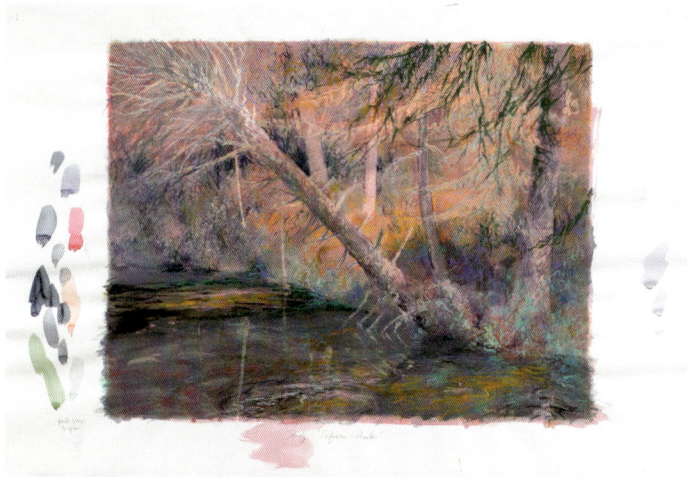

*Infusion – Amber, Tay River AB*, 1999
oil on canvas
60 x 80 inches (152.4 x 203.2 cm)

*Infusion – Amber, Tay River AB* (*Study*), 1999
mixed media on paper
18 x 24 inches (45.72 x 60.96 cm)

*Light Burst – Dark Forest* (*Study*), 2000
charcoal on paper
19 x 23 inches (48.26 x 58.42 cm)

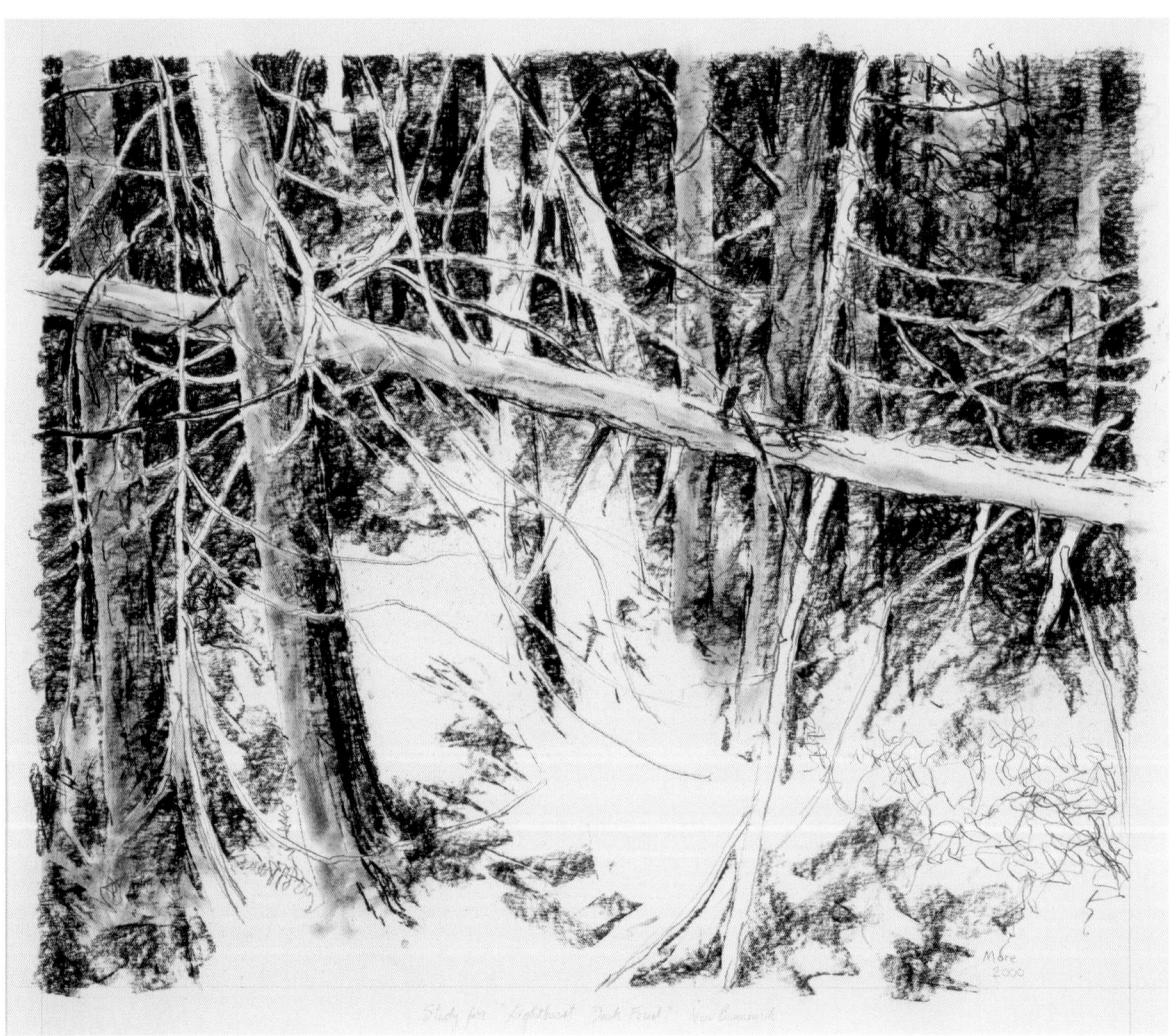

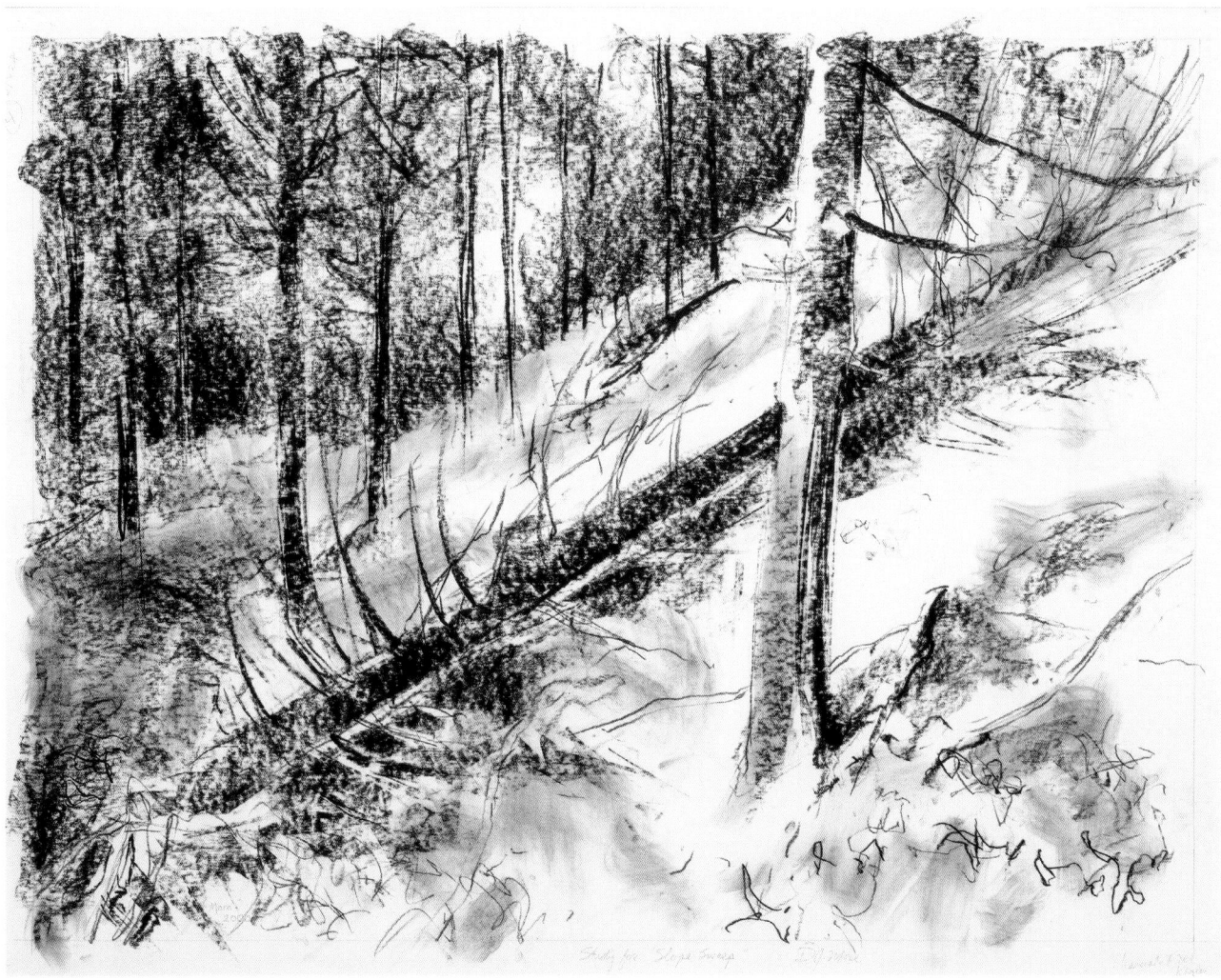

*Slope Sweep* (*Study*), 2000
charcoal on paper
21 x 28 inches
(53.34 x 71.12 cm)

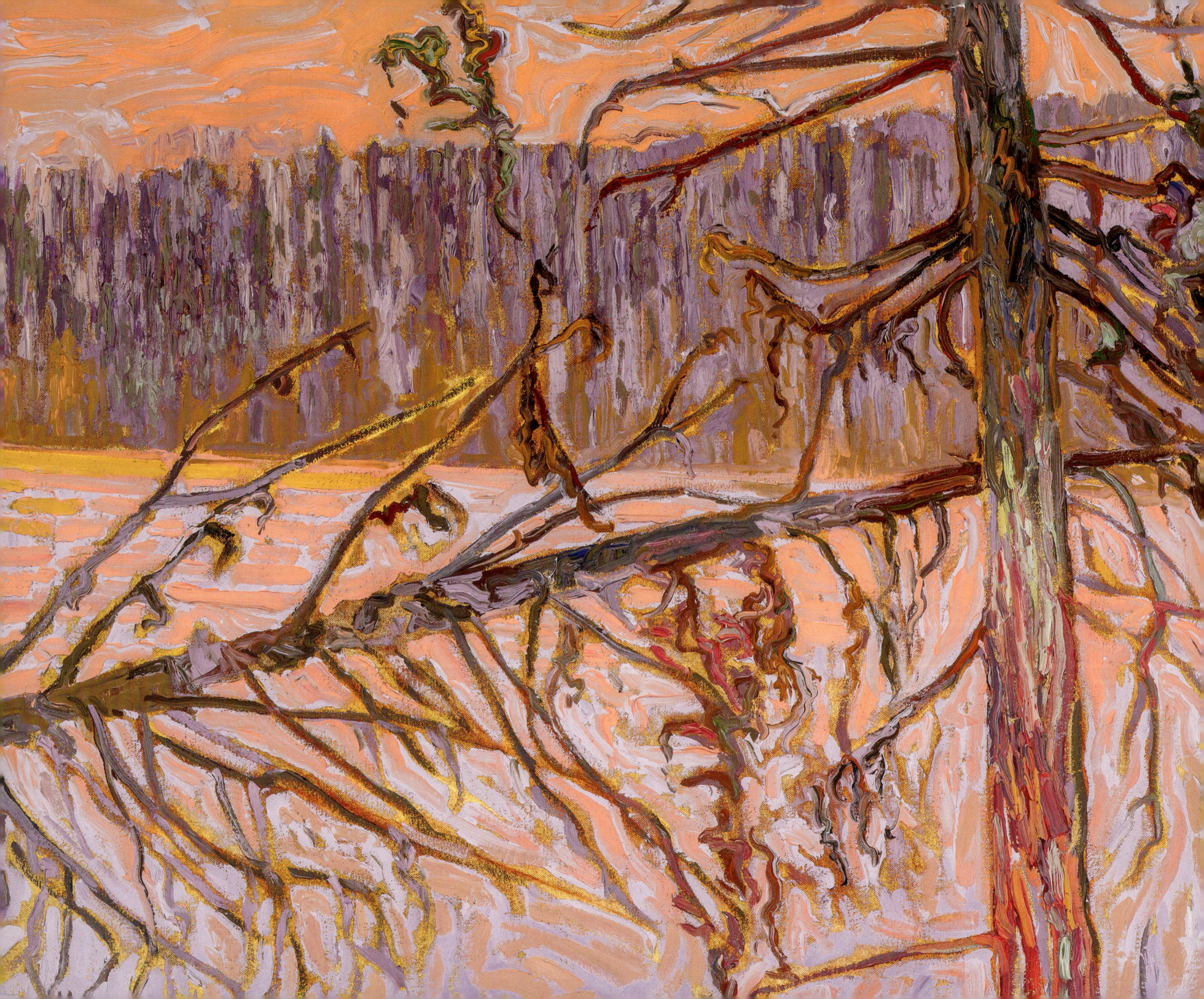

# GHOSTLY FORESTS, UNCERTAIN SKIES

*"…through my career, the 'Garden' has played a role in the way I see the landscape in general. The touring exhibition* **Forest–Fade to Silent** *in the early 90's dealt with the reality of acid rain in the eastern forest…I think we all see nature at it's untouched as the biggest and best part of the garden we call Earth."*

DAVID MORE (Interview, *Red Deer Express*, 2012)[1]

Near the end of the 1980s, David and Yvette noticed something different in her home province of New Brunswick. The silence in its forests was startling. Birds and squirrels were absent; the lakes empty of fish and other life. As for the trees, they were dying from the bottom up. Acid rain? Yes, according to the local rangers.

Determined to respond, More produced a powerful series of artworks with cinematographic titles like *Fade to Grey* and the chilling *Fade to Black*. In Banff, the Whyte Museum of the Canadian Rockies organized a two-and-a-half-year national tour of *Forest–Fade to Silent*. Featuring thirty-six paintings and mixed media works, the exhibit was seen in the public galleries of ten Canadian towns and cities. Critics noticed how the series played off the legacy of The Group of Seven so admired by More.[2] But with its acrid colours and skeletal treatment of the forest, this was a ghostly wilderness which would be unrecognizable to the canoe-paddling Tom Thomson. Rather than a celebratory style with beautiful complementary colours, noted one critic, the artist's choice of colour "fit together in an eerie and uncomfortable union." As a body of exhibited work, *Forest–Fade to Silent* was prescient.

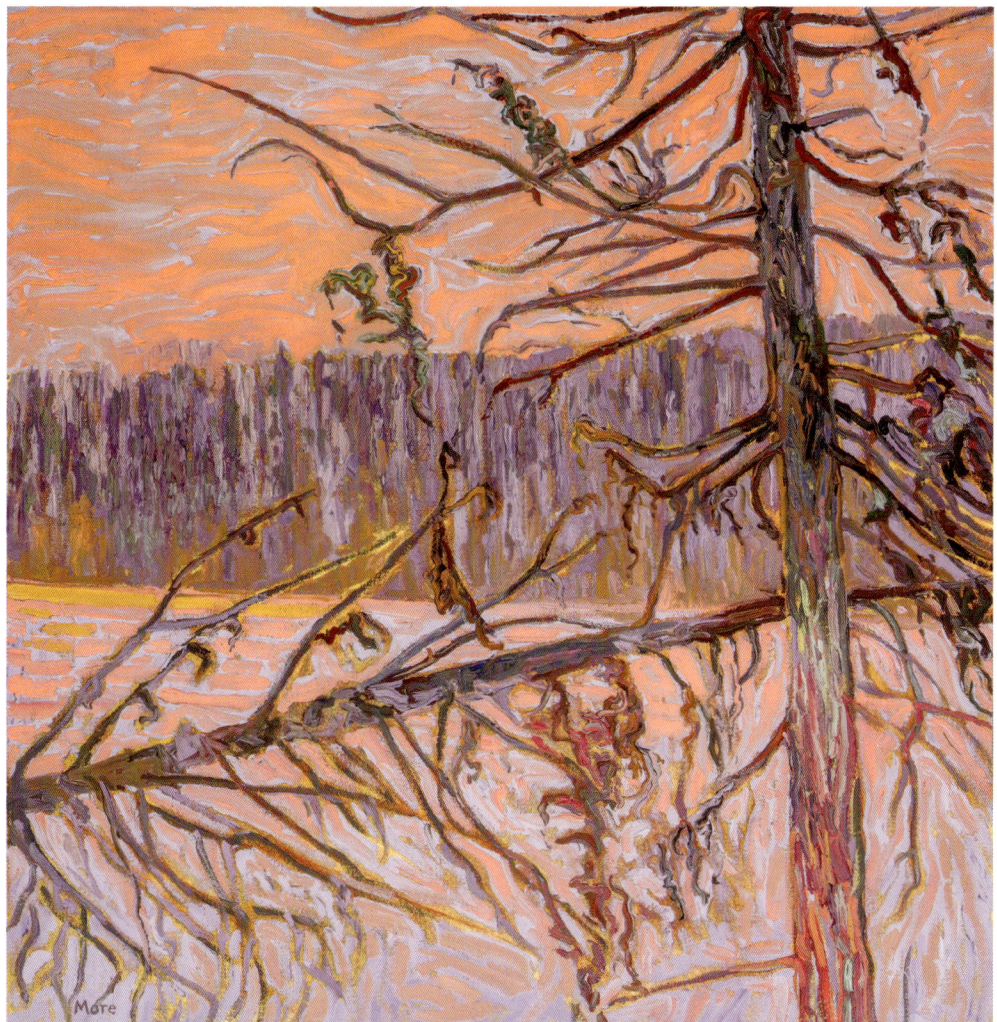

*Lake of Vapours*, 1990
oil on canvas
30 x 30 inches (76.2 x 76.2 cm)

Detail of *Lake of Vapours*, 1990 on page 46.

*New Brunswick Forest, Fade to Grey II,*
1990
oil on canvas
30 x 30 inches (76.2 x 76.2 cm)

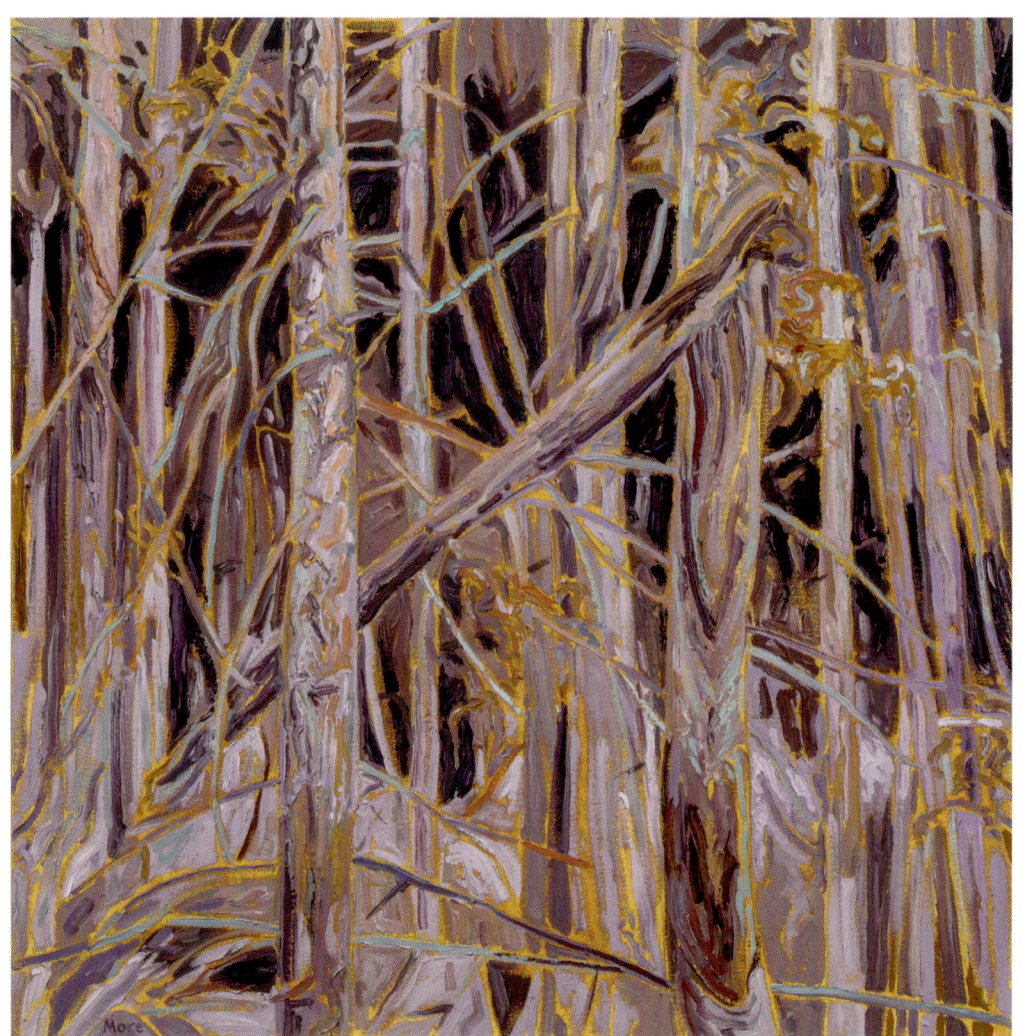

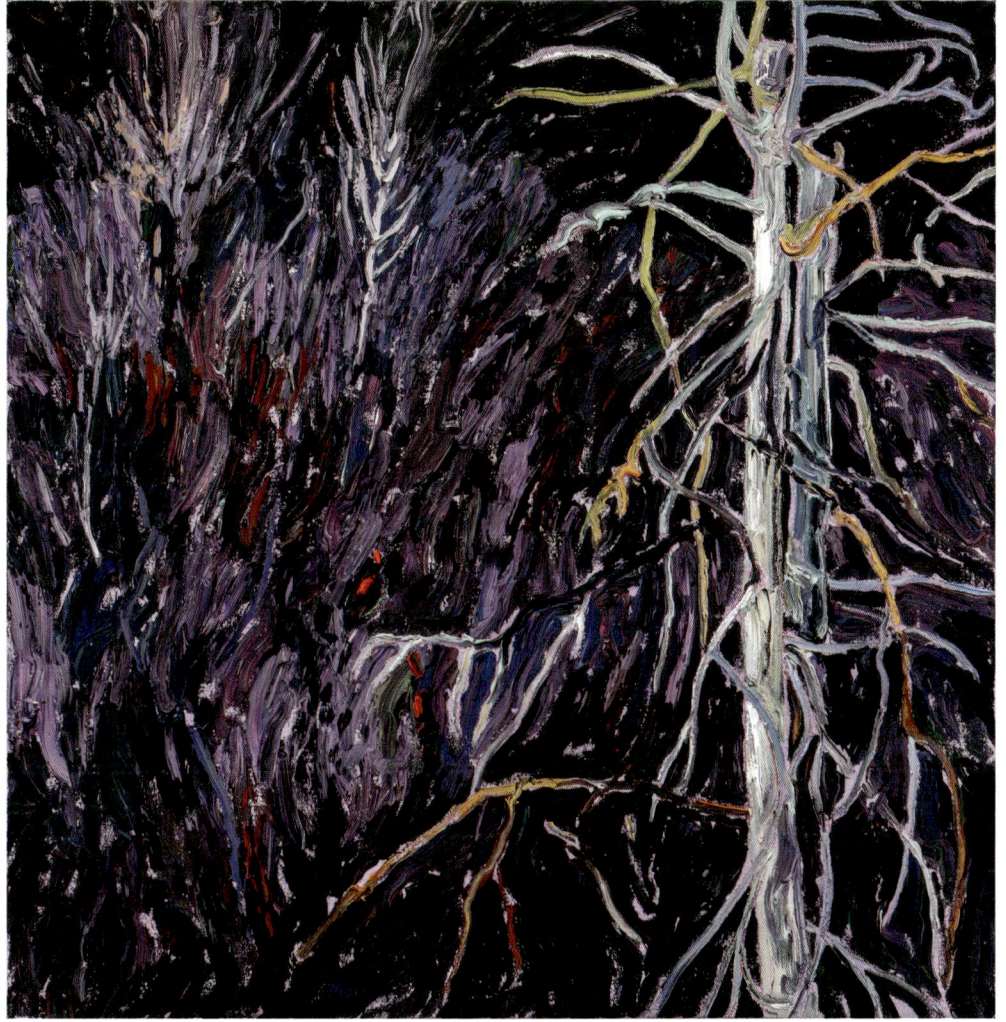

*New Brunswick Forest, Fade to Black V,*
1990
oil on canvas
30 x 30 inches (76.2 x 76.2 cm)

*Study for Vapour Trails, Vapour Trees #1*, 1989
mixed media on paper
18 x 18 inches (54.72 x 45.72 cm)

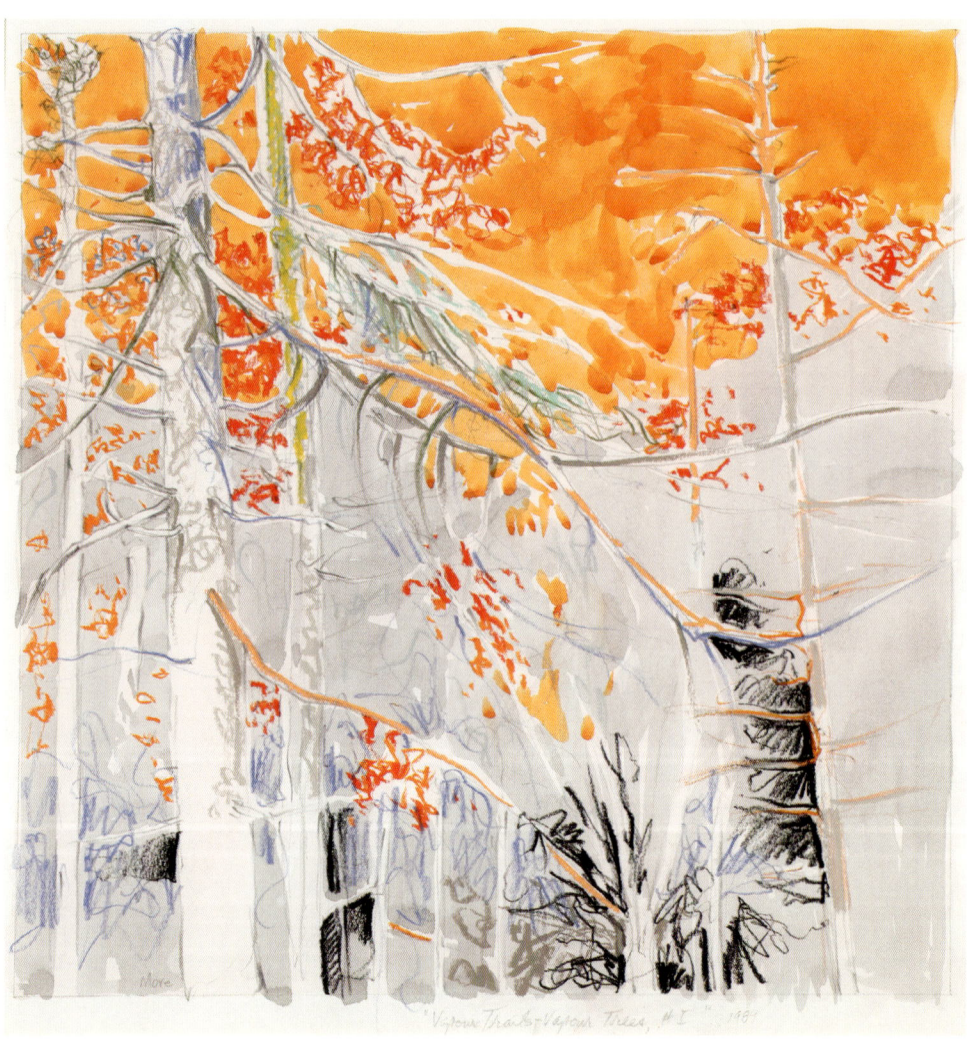

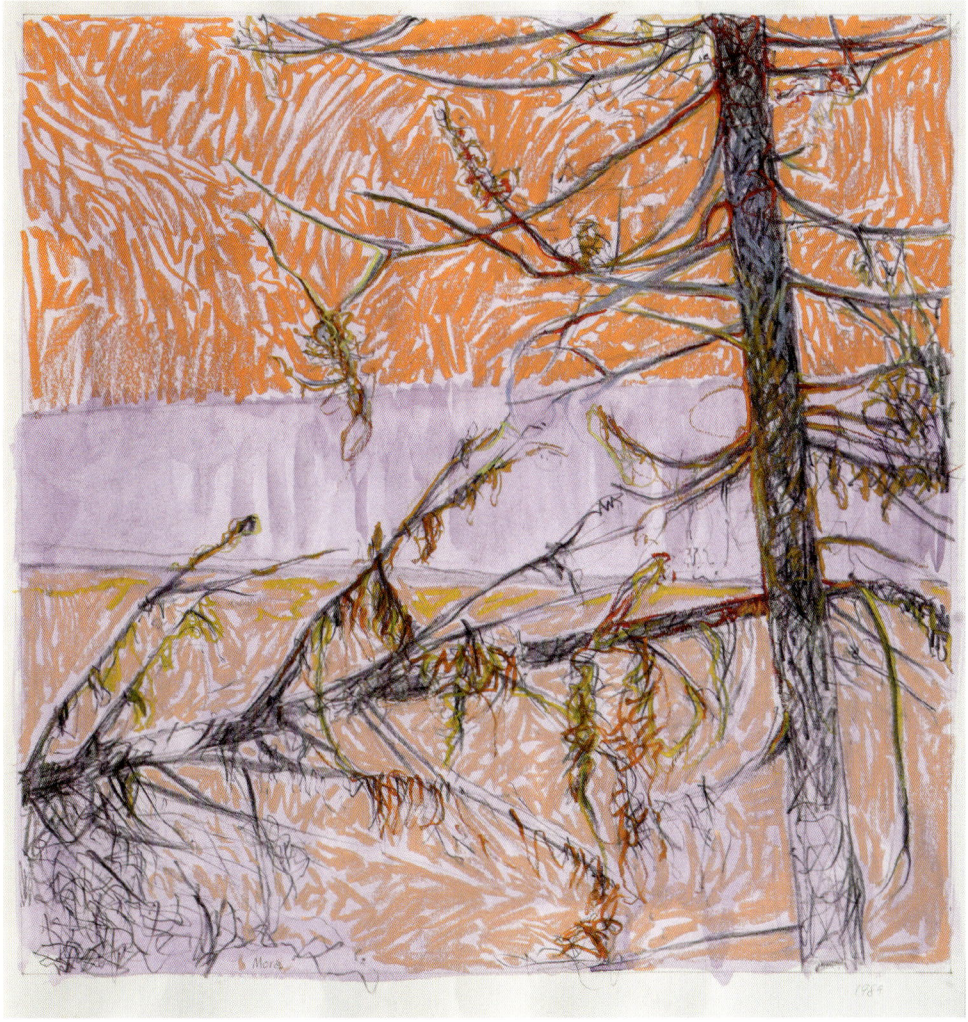

*Study for Lake of Vapours*, 1989
mixed media on paper
18 x 18 inches (54.72 x 45.72 cm)

*"That's our identity, isn't it?"*

DAVID MORE, *The Medicine Hat News*[3]

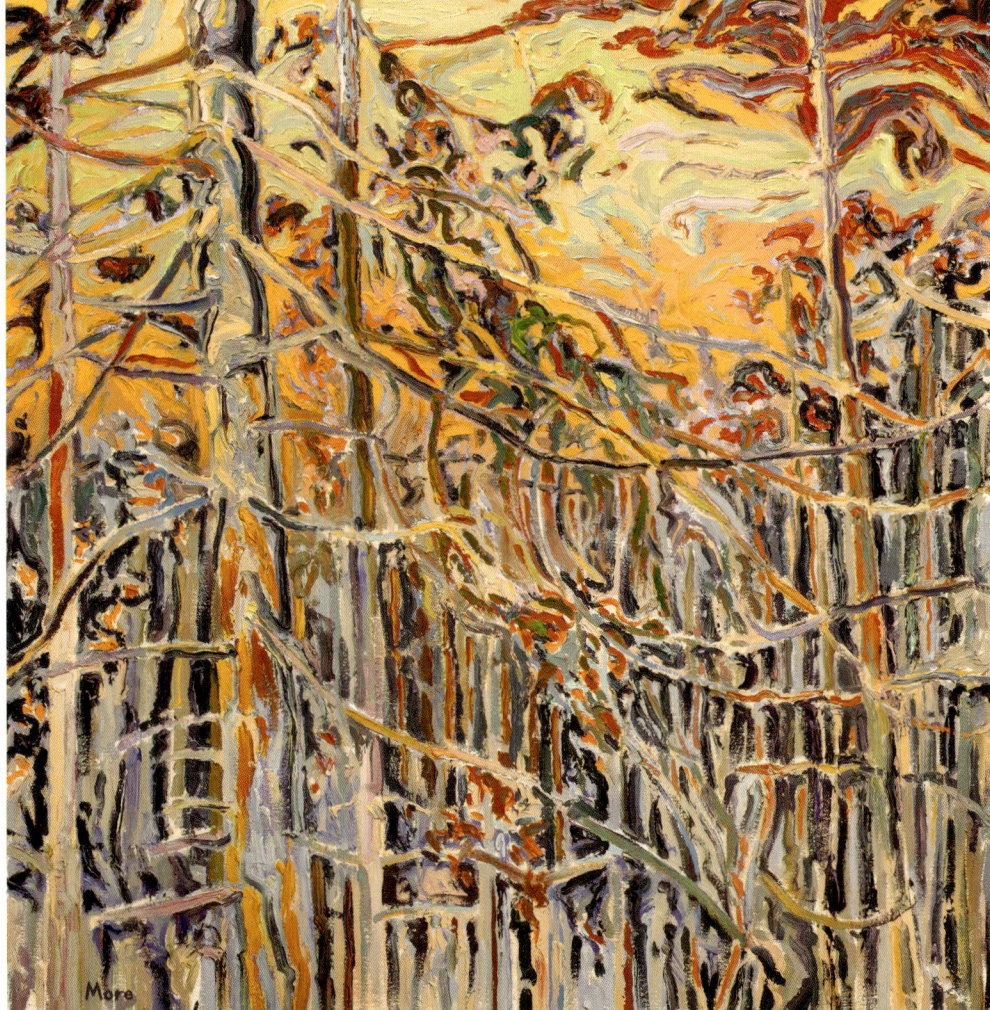

*Vapour Trails, Vapour Trees*, 1990
oil on canvas
30 x 30 inches (76.2 x 76.2 cm)

"With climate change has come a dramatic shift to the dynamics of my sky works. On July 14, 2000, I was painting just north of Benalto and focused on a mass of clouds forming above a canola field. The cloud built heavily as the hours wore on. About halfway through the painting I felt a sudden compulsion and reached onto my palette with a cloth and swept up a gob of cadmium red and smeared it onto the image of the cloud. I was startled by my action, seemingly coming from somewhere beyond me. Fitfully, I continued the painting, and the cloud mass changed direction, moving southeastward. Within an hour the cloud had become a massive tornado, killing 12 people at Pine Lake.

*I had a great difficulty with skies after that. Many of my sky images after 2000 are tormented, with clashing colours and forms. Something that I once held in reverence had become a demon. In the decade that followed and since, many more violent storms have marched across the lands as the climate shifts. The 2005 series initially called "Into a Greater Distance" (later with additions, called "Vanishing Point") was my attempt to address the warning we are receiving...and in many instances, to our peril, ignoring."*

DAVID MORE (Studio Notes)[4]

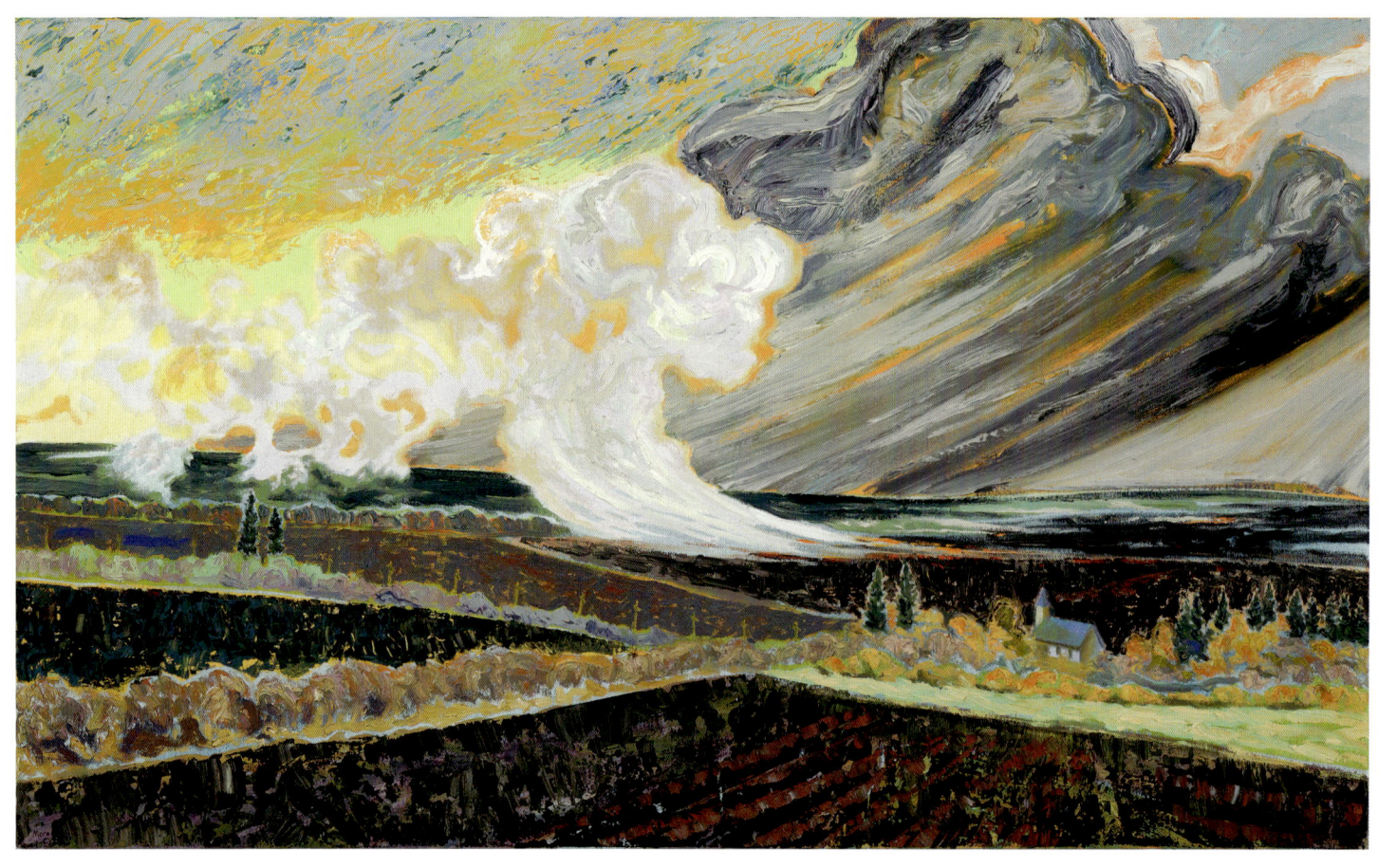

*Fire & Hope* (central Alberta), 2010
oil on canvas
24 x 40 inches (60.96 x 1010.6 cm)

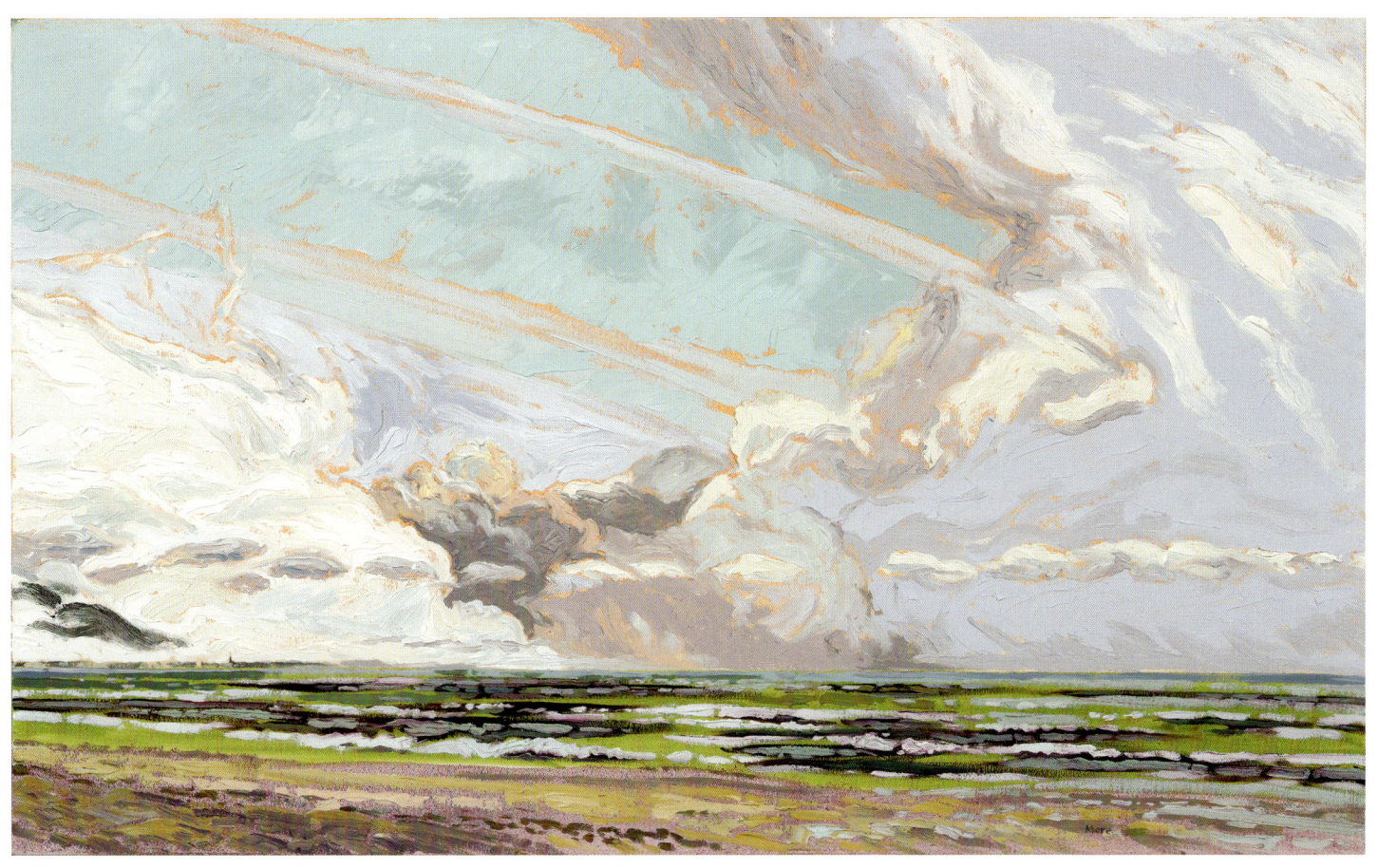

*Spires Above Petit Rocher* (New Brunswick), 2008
oil on canvas
24 x 40 inches (60.96 x 1010.6 cm)

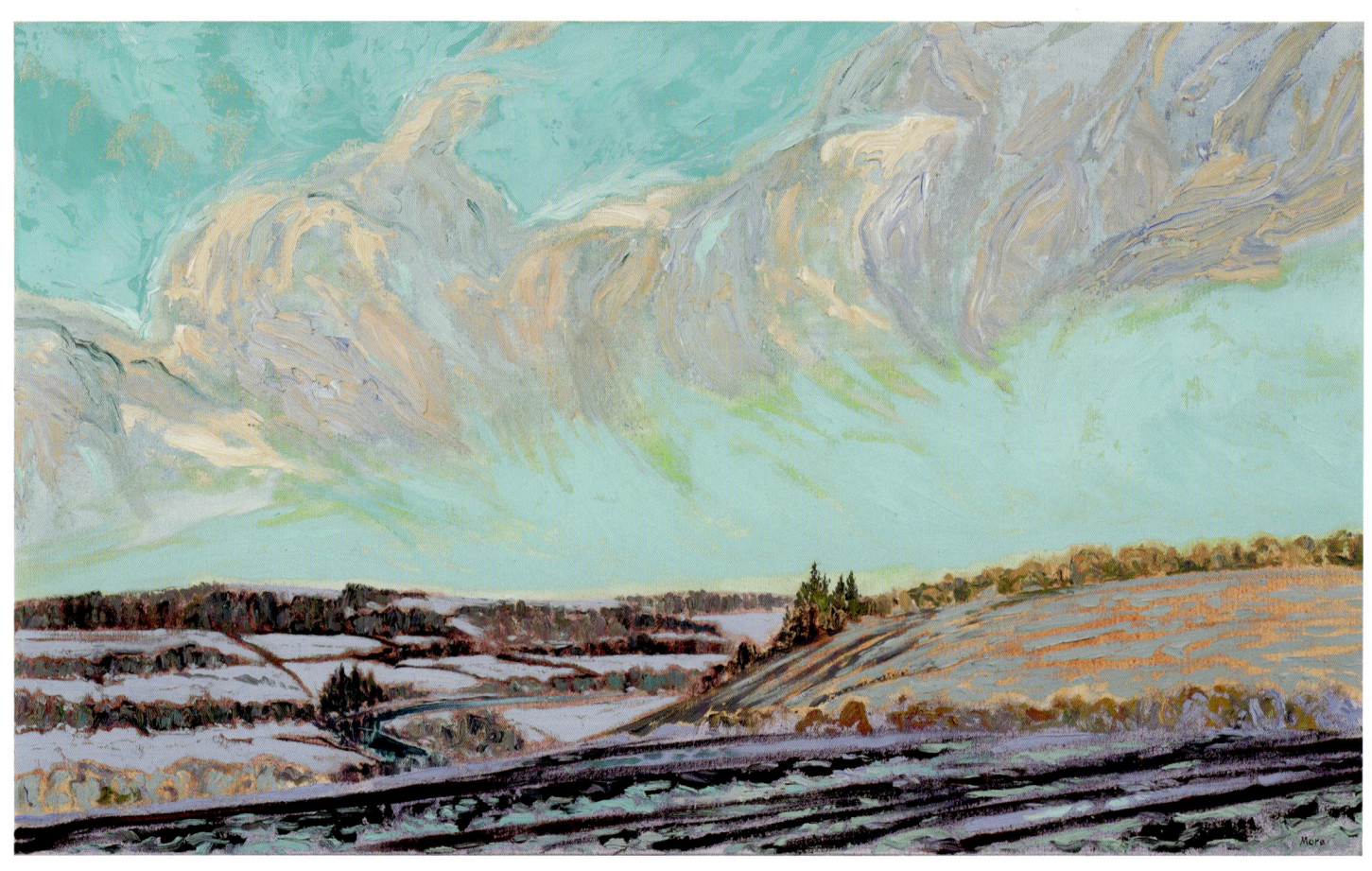

*Escarpment* (central Alberta), 2010
oil on canvas
24 x 40 inches (60.96 x 1010.6 cm)

*"Nowhere is a 'sense of place' more clearly evoked than by the big uncertain skies of prairie and sea. Clouds are the dominating element, and their evocation by David More is almost an emotional one. Colour is another element, with the artist pushing his palette to dramatic heights. Despite their realism, Sky Cathedrals also recalls the painter's training in the early 1970s when abstraction was a dominant mode of expression in Canadian art."*

DAVID MORE: A PAINTER'S GIFT, Red Deer Museum + Art Gallery[5]

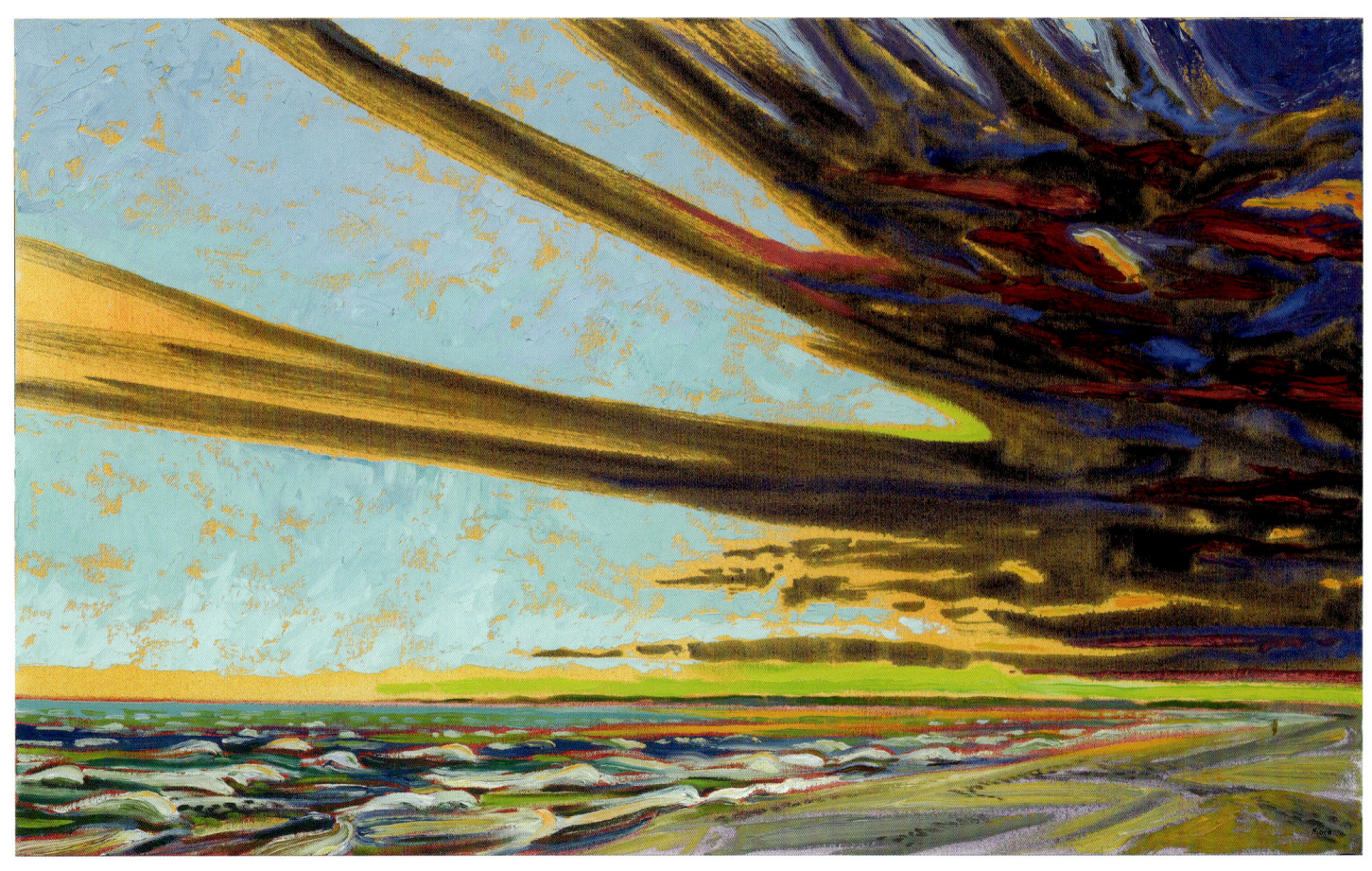

*Figure on a Shore* (New Brunswick) 2010
oil on canvas
24 x 40 inches (60.96 x 101.6 cm)
Detail of *Figure on a Shore* (New Brunswick) 2010 on page 63.

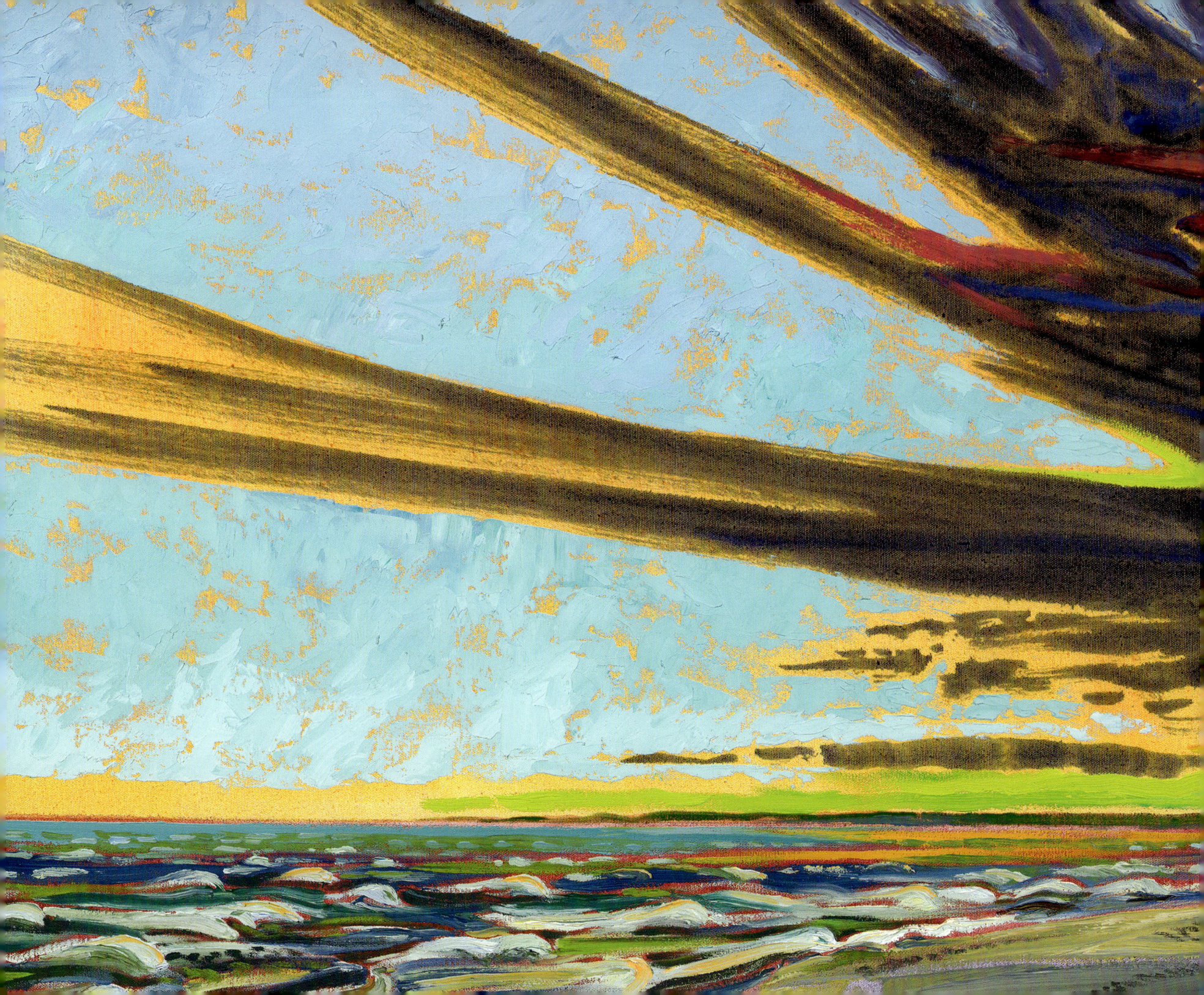

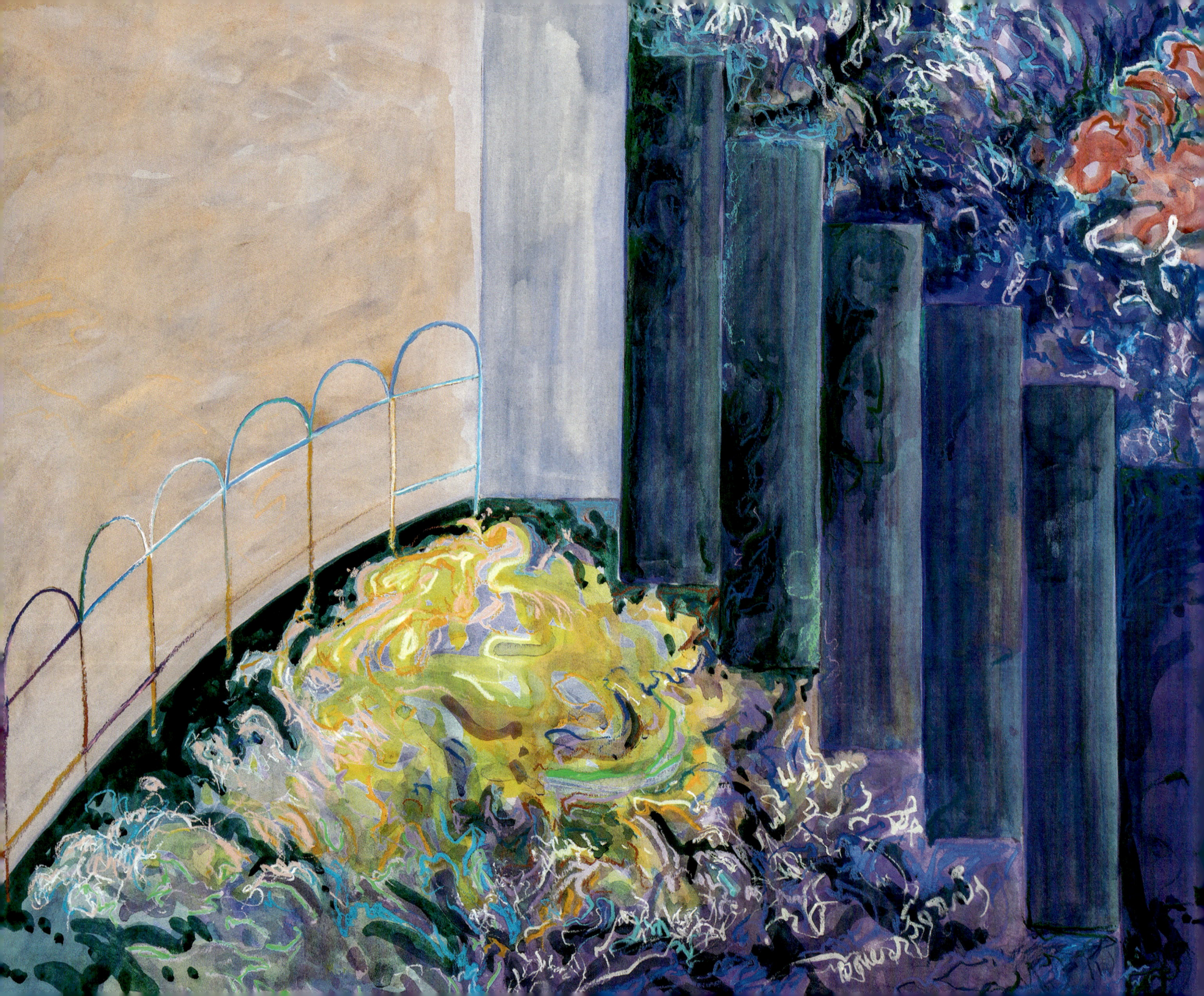

# THE IGNITION OF MEMORY,
# PART ONE: THE GARDEN CEREMONY

*"Brought on by a need to seek solace at a time of personal difficulty from a disintegrating marriage,* **Garden Ceremony** *led me to meditative wanderings in the sanctuary of gardens and parks. The resulting imagery was, and continues to expand upon, the reflective state of mind inspired by those imaginary gardens."*

DAVID MORE (STUDIO NOTES)[1]

Garden stairs and walks, ornamental architecture and garden squares, clipped hedges and thoughtfully placed trees, these places, including some which are abandoned, are the most personal of David More's landscapes. Rather than a pictorial representation of an actual garden or park, the canvases and works on paper or museum board are acts of commemoration–a ceremonial nod to events and travels in the artist's life when only the garden could provide refuge or a sense of belonging. Maybe the actual garden site is not so important, but in the Red Deer & District Museum Society Art Collection, Rio de Janeiro, Brazil, Hamilton, Ontario, Cochin (Kochi), India, and an unusual graveyard of Second World War planes served as sources of inspiration, all reimagined by the artist.

In 1992, David and Yvette travelled to the lush state of Kerala on the southwest coast of India. After the success of More's travelling exhibition, *Forest–Fade to Silent*, the formal gardens found in old palace grounds around Cochin (Kochi) provided a new and refreshing connection to the garden theme. As a harbinger of good luck, an elegantly designed *rangoli* on the floor in the foreground of *Garden Ceremony with India Forms – Rangoli #1* welcomes the viewer. Closer to home, *Garden Passage XI* and *XII* invite us for further exploration. Whether in India or in the historic Red Deer neighbourhood of Waskasoo–where such well-trodden steps are often found–they represent sites transformed by a flattened perspective, abstracted elements, patterns, and symbolic colour.

*Garden Passage XI*, 1983
mixed media on board
32 x 32 inches (81.28 x 81.28 cm)

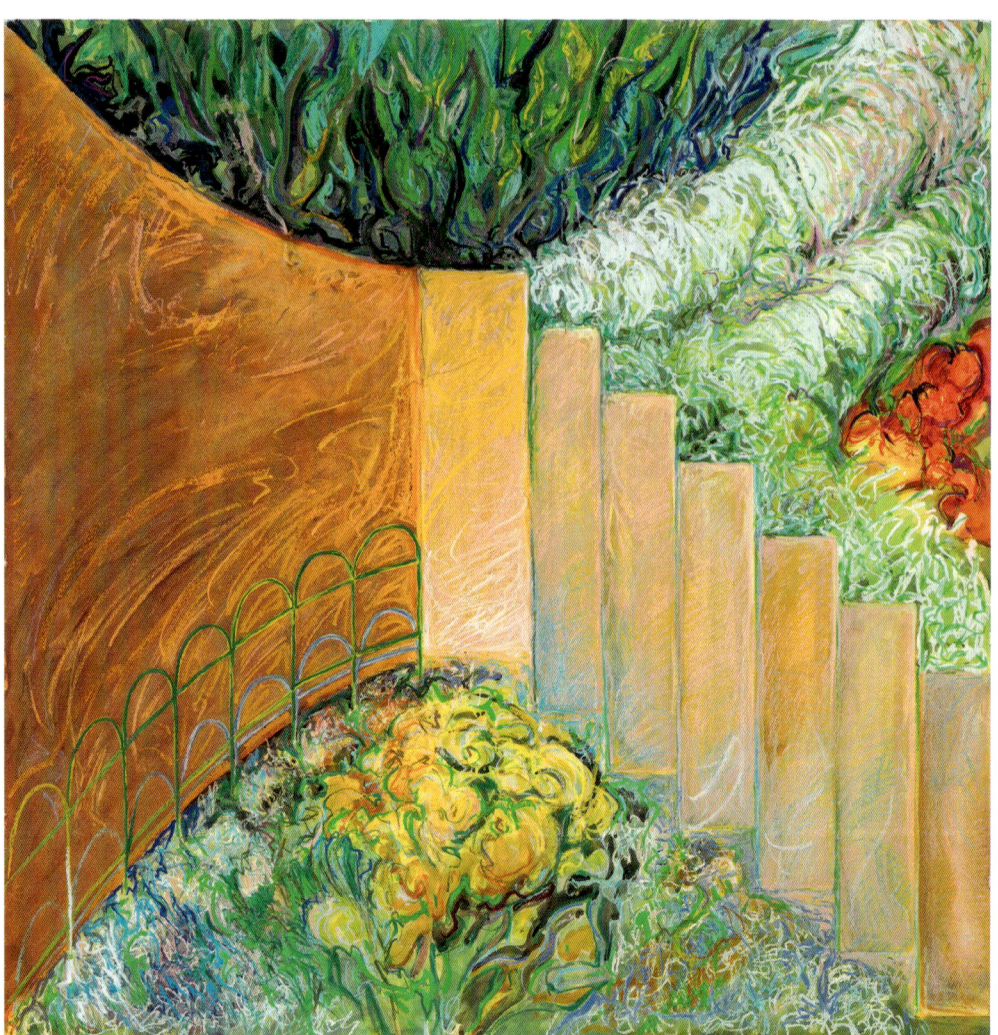

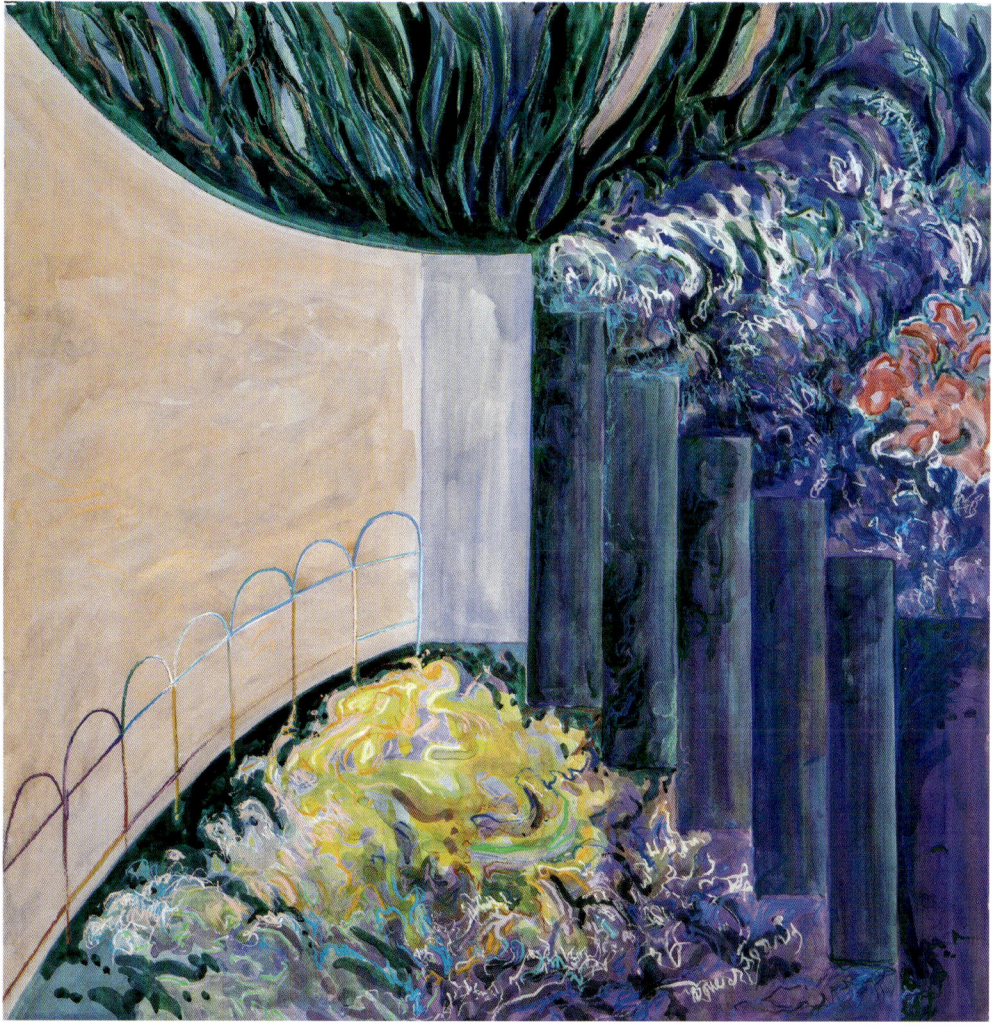

*Garden Passage XII*, 1983
mixed media on board
32 x 32 inches (81.28 x 81.28 cm)
Detail of *Garden Passage XII*, 1983 on
page 64.

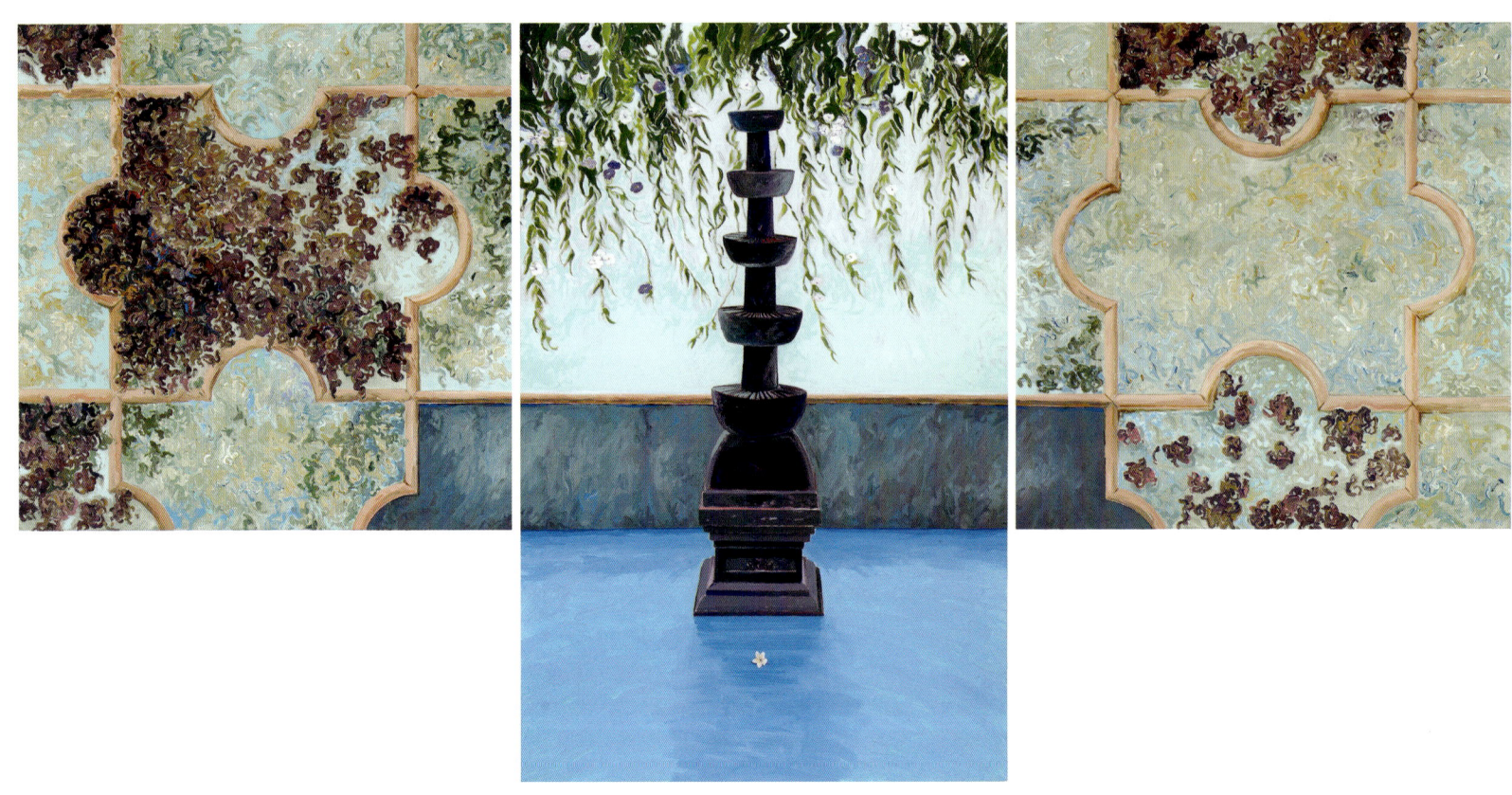

*Garden Ceremony with India Forms – Cochin #1*, 1995
Acrylic on canvas (triptych)
5.7 x 10 feet (1.737 x 3.048 metres)

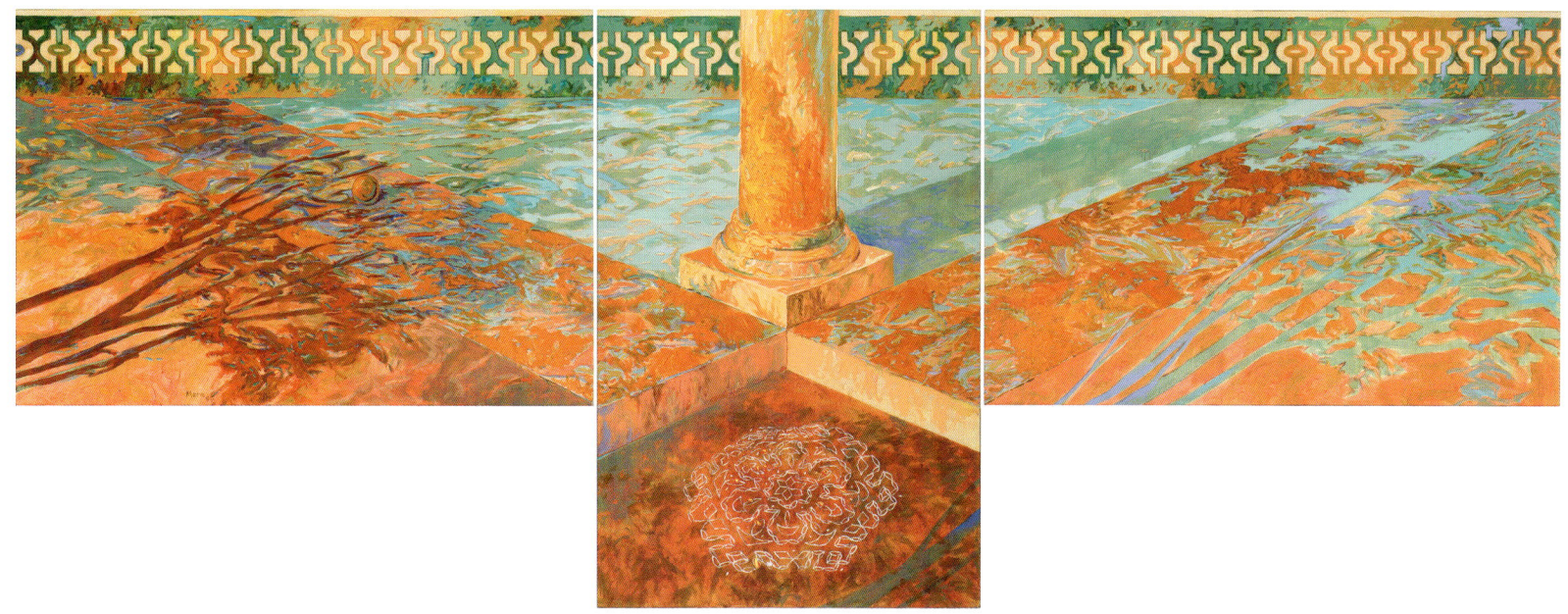

*Garden Ceremony with India Forms – Rangoli #1*, 1995
Acrylic on canvas (triptych)
5 x 13.3 feet (1.5 x 4.05 metres)

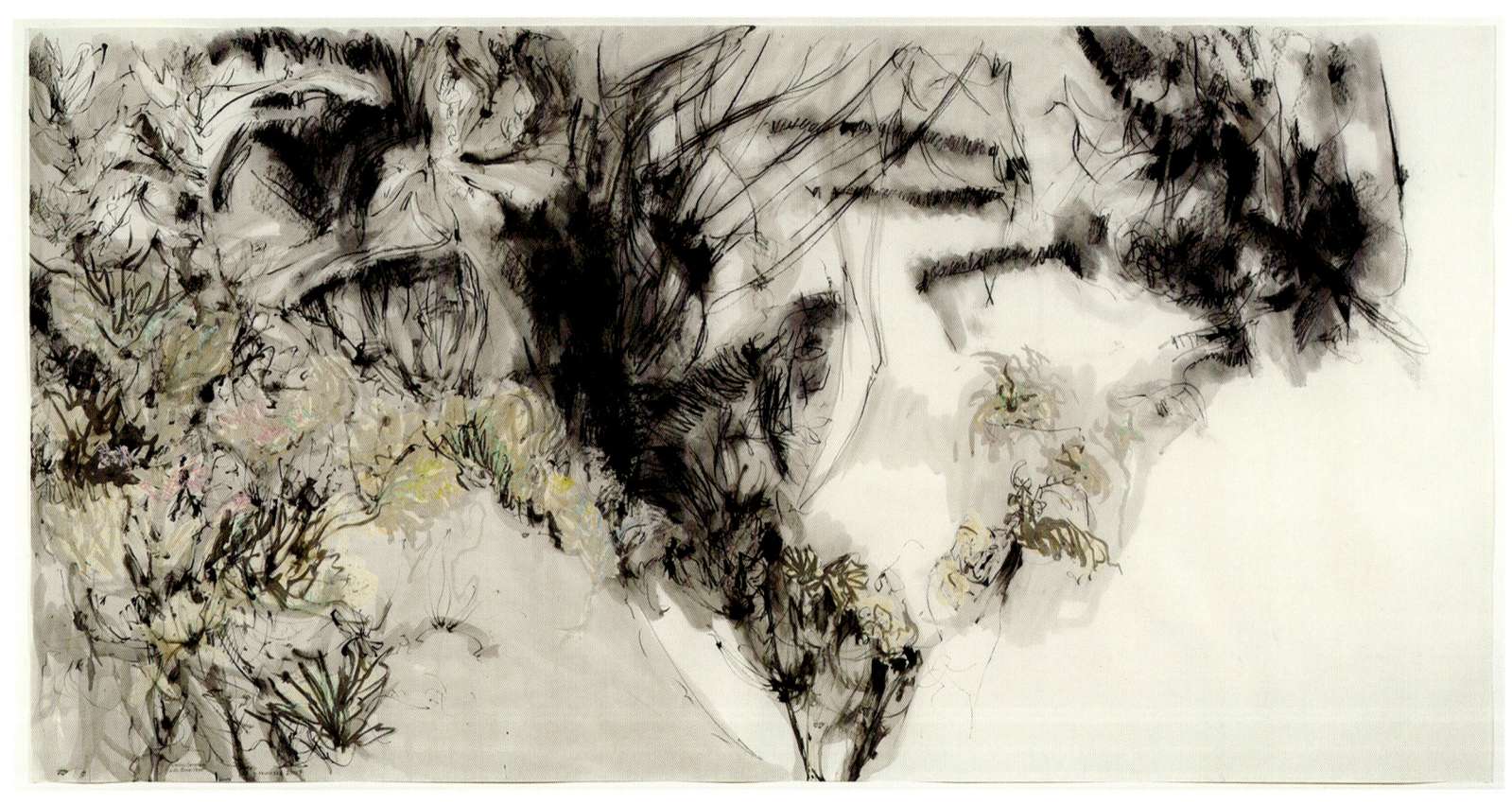

*Garden Ceremony with Snow Steps*, 1977–2007
mixed media on paper
48 x 96 inches (1221 x 242 cm)

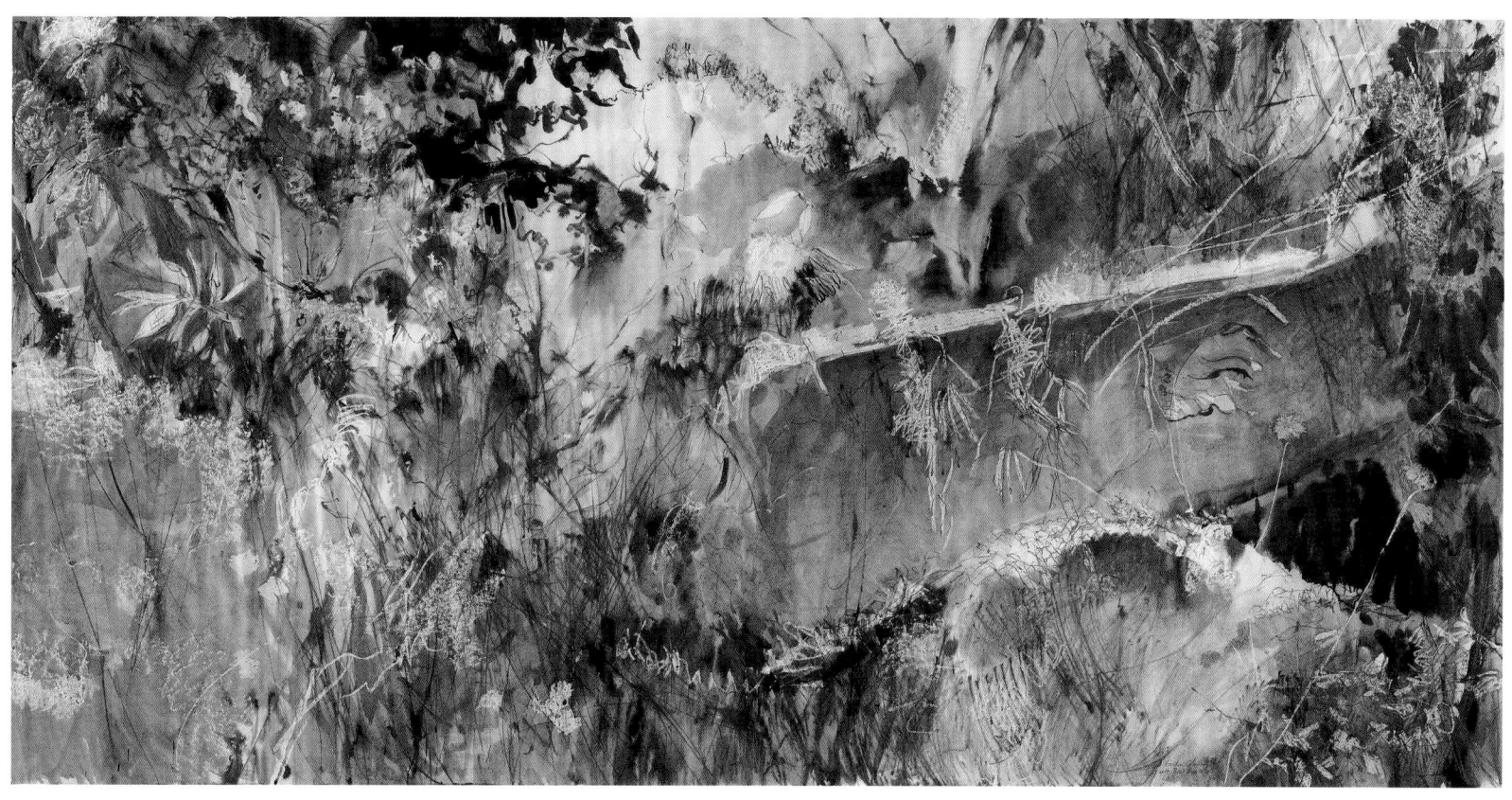

*The Garden Ceremony with Brazilian Wall*, 1977
mixed media on paper
48 x 96 inches (121 x 242 cm)
Detail of *The Garden Ceremony with Brazilian Wall*, 1977 on page 74.

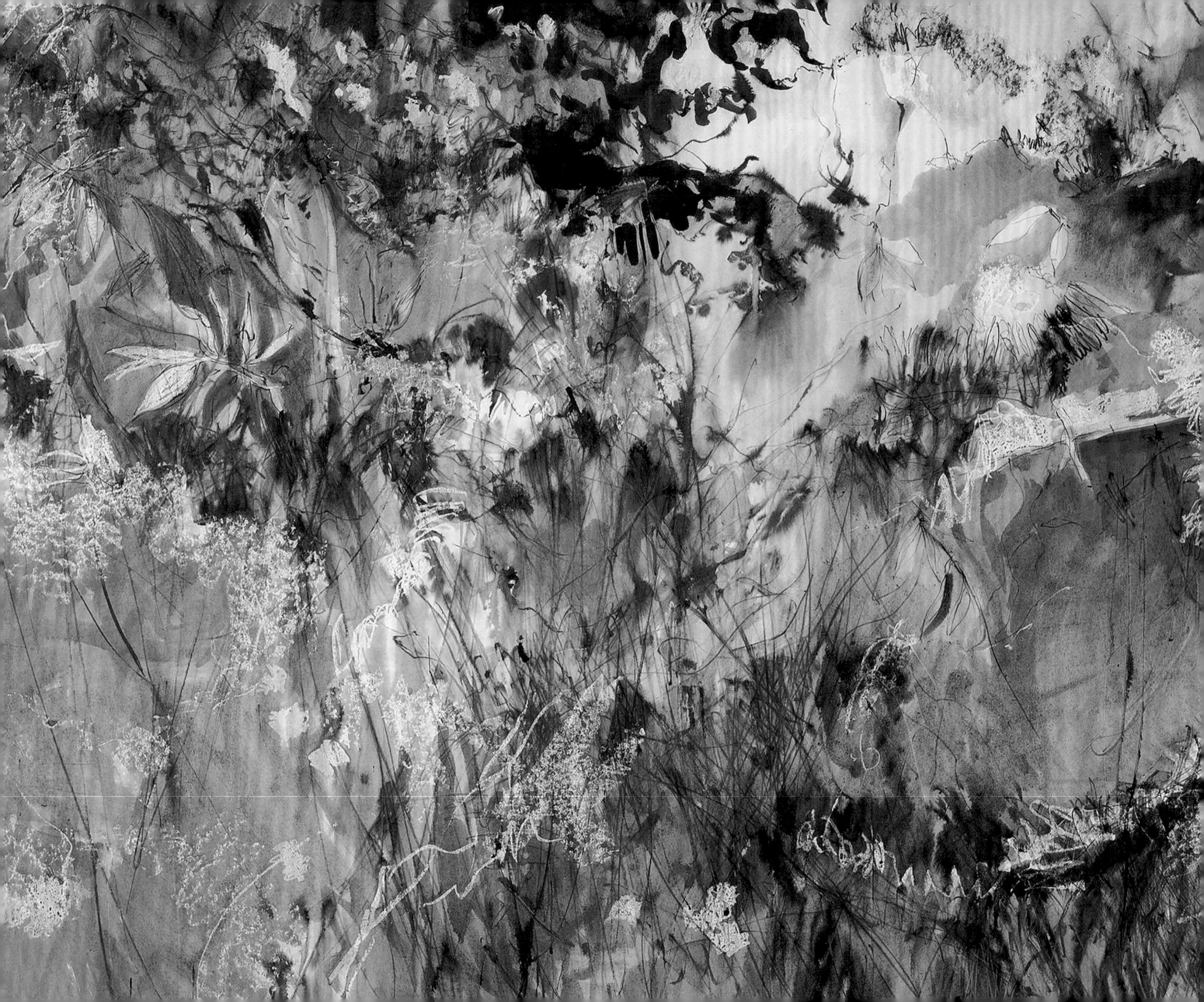

*"At the base of a mountain where a street of gold meets the favela's crude path, where promise meets poverty, a garden forms..."*

DAVID MORE (*The Garden Ceremony*)[2]

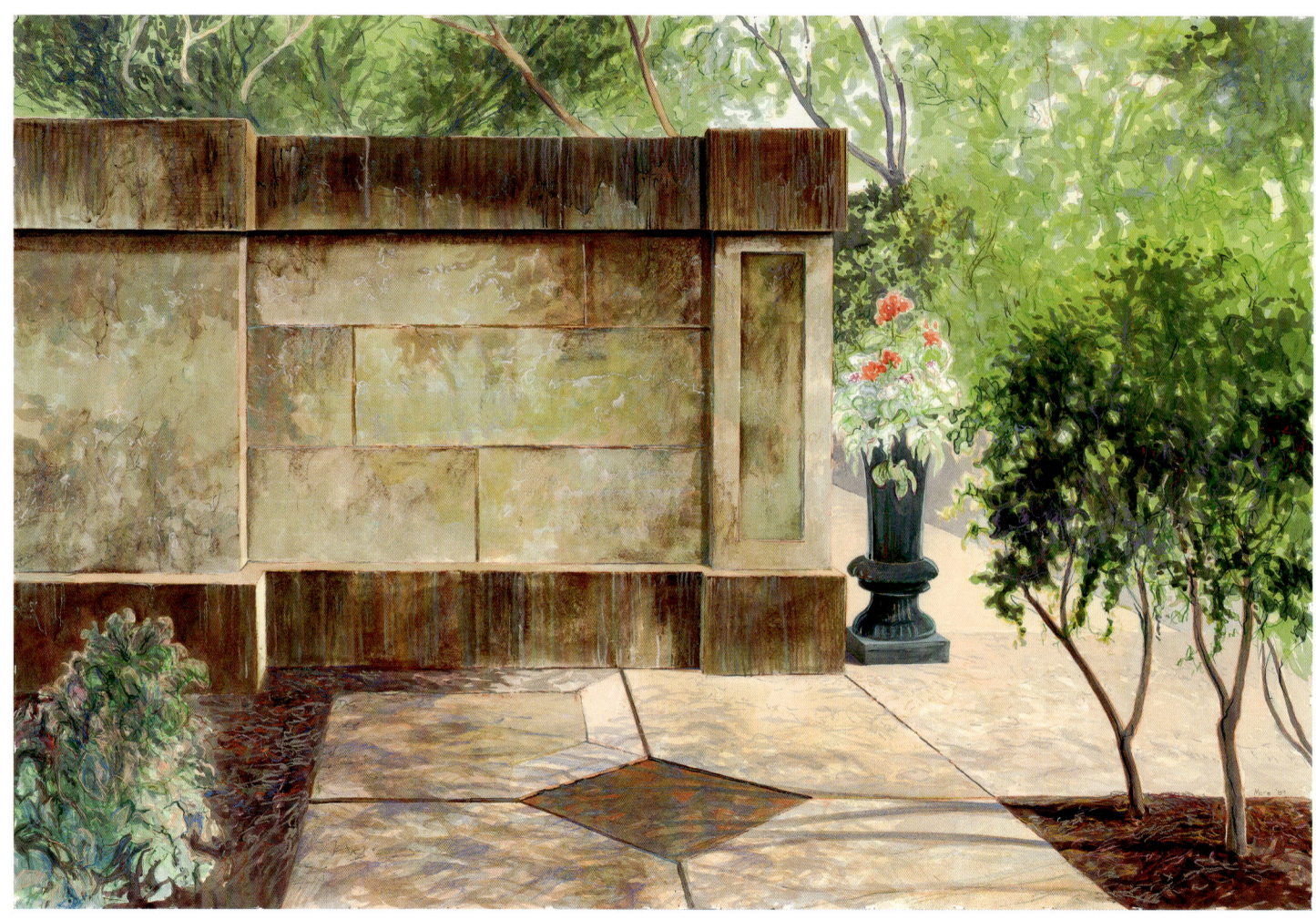

*Garden Ceremony with Red Diamond*, 1989
mixed media on museum board
40 x 60 inches (101.6 x 152.4 cm)

*"Painter Mary Pratt speaks of how her youthful world was that of her family's back garden in Fredericton. It was the universe that shaped her imagination and formed her vision. Claude Monet brought all of his aesthetic sensibilities into one garden art piece–his garden at Giverny in France. His life had become a garden; his garden had become his life. Together they allowed him to share his magnificent reflection upon it all."*

DAVID MORE (*…of Gardens*)[3]

## War's Garden

Taking David More a year to build and paint each monumental artwork, the two acrylic-on-wood paintings from the *War's Garden* series imagine an era now only faintly recalled. Wing-shaped, they are inspired by More's own childhood memories of a nearby military airfield in Penhold, Alberta, his mother's own involvement in Britain's Women's Royal Air Force, and the remnants of Second World War training planes he saw as a young boy. These remnants had fabled aircraft names like Spitfire and Corsair.

As shaped paintings, they serve as the surface upon which the artist has painted some of his most lyrical and romantic gardens, as in *Spitfire Steps*. The gardens are, of course, a haven or a place of contemplation. In one instance–*Night Garden, Corsair, Descending Over Water*–no garden can be seen, only the calm darkened waters of a garden pond painted on the gullwing shape of an aircraft high above in the sky.

This juxtaposition between the peace and quiet of a garden and the destructive aircraft of war is another example of how the garden theme is carried beyond its usual, appealing associations. Not intended to be merely descriptive, these sites as interpreted and visualized by David More are uniquely idiosyncratic.

*Night Garden, Corsair, Descending Over Water*, 2007
acrylic on wood
62 inches (1.57 metres) x 18 feet (5.49 metres)
Collection of the Artist

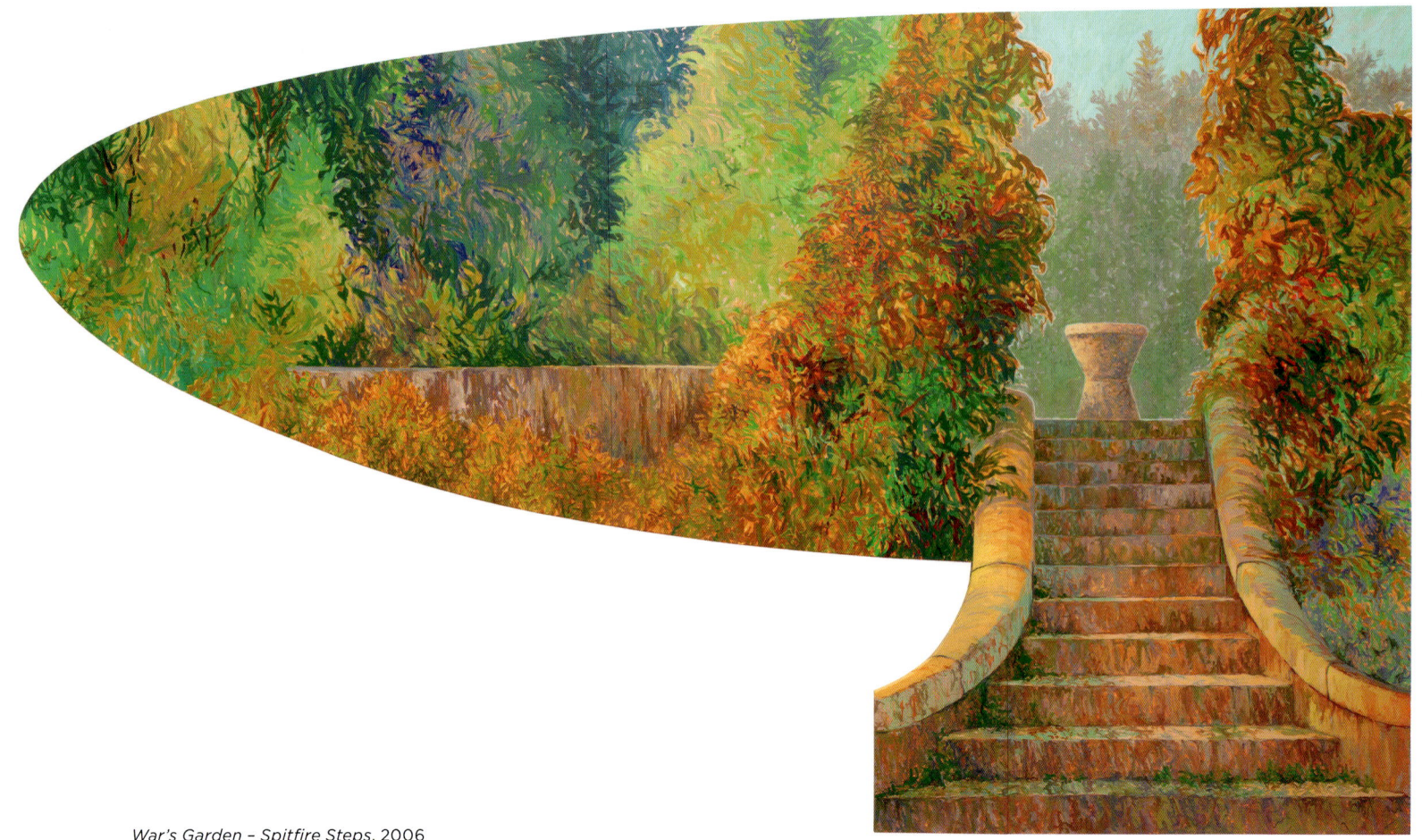

*War's Garden – Spitfire Steps*, 2006
acrylic on wood (diptych)
8 feet (2.44 metres) x 14 feet, 9 inches (4.37 metres)
Collection of the Artist

*"The sublimely beautiful wing shape of a Spitfire fuses with English garden steps of my mother's youth. The layers of foliage and stone wall mimic the camouflage patterns of my mother's air force days. The steps rise up to another level and the garden birdbath of my childhood in Red Deer, ten thousand miles and a sanctuary of years later."*

DAVID MORE (*The Garden Ceremony*)[4]

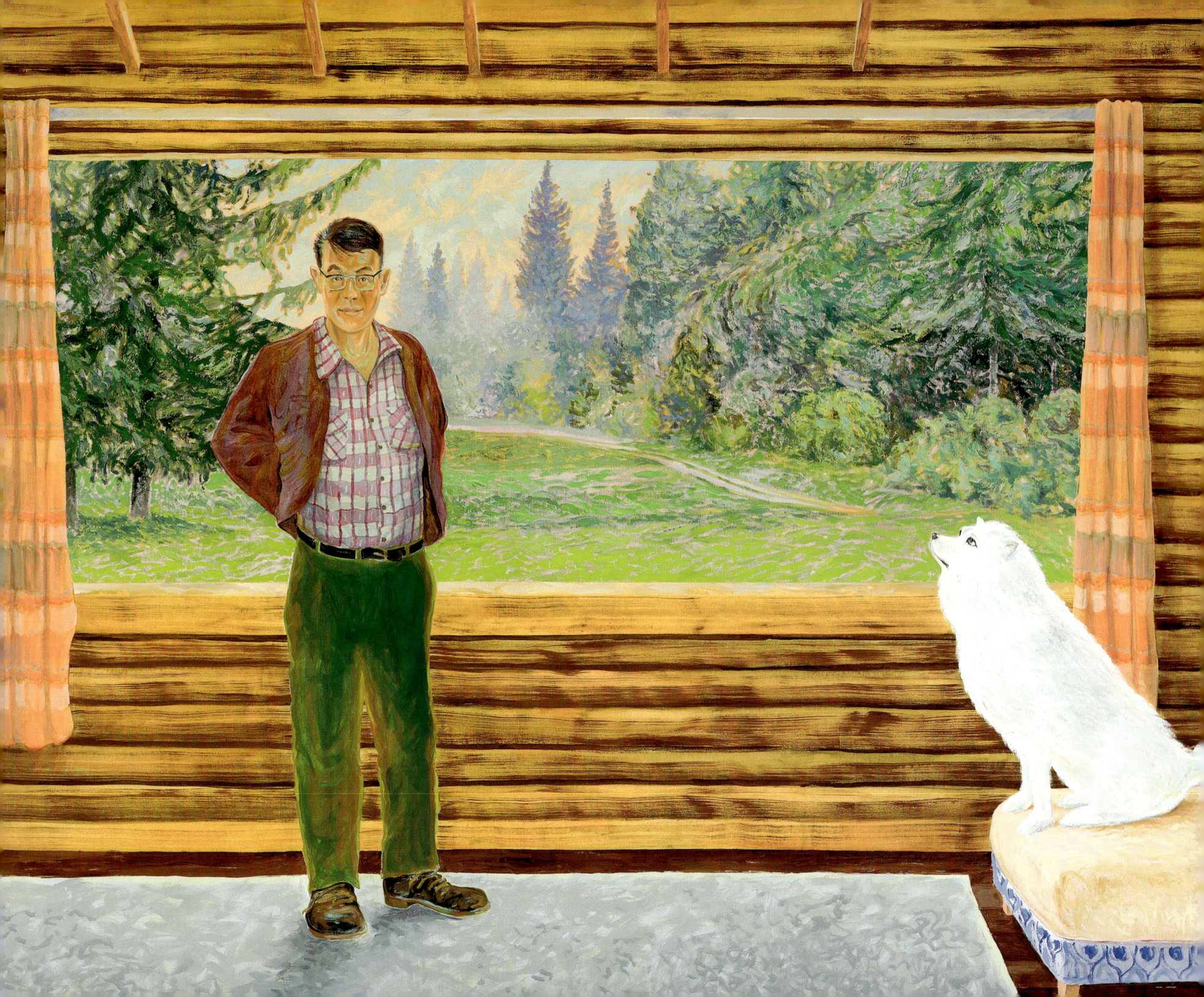

# THE IGNITION OF MEMORY, PART TWO: CANADIAN WINDOW

*"While living on Vancouver Island, Yvette & I met a number of fascinating people and were invited to their homes. I was struck by how often people's picture window was a remarkable landscape. I asked these folks if they would pose for photographs, in any manner they chose, in front of 'their' landscape, and I began a series of drawings."*

DAVID MORE (Studio Notes)[1]

In the *Canadian Window* series, landscape and treasured relationships are interwoven around the theme of the picture window. Functionally, as a large pane of glass, a window provides not just a source of light but also a *view*. Begun three decades ago and with many hiatuses in between, this body of work reveals a different side of More's creative personality: his interest in people and their personal connections to the landscapes and/or gardens they love.

Inspired in the 1970s by David Hockney's *Mr & Mrs Smith and Percy*, More was impressed with the British artist's portrayal of a young couple and their cat, Percy,[2] and Hockney's careful staging of them in front of a balustrade with partly-opened window-shutters. To More, Hockney's acrylic on canvas signified a very modern approach to portraiture.[3] But within a Canadian context, this idea developed into a room with a more serious, wide-open view–a view onto a landscape or garden which took them visually and psychologically into a wider world.

Aside from expanding on the composition, More's process took a different route. Treating the landscape or garden as a painting within a painting, he taped off the window frame and used oil paint to realise the outdoor scene. In contrast, for the interior scene, he applied thin layers of acrylic to its subjects. Which was more important? Both, each a different side of the same coin.

Also critical to the process and final composition were the graphite studies. The three examples provided in this chapter illustrate a singularly adept individual whose preliminary drawings exuded a "delicious sensitivity."[4] Many drawings went into the creation of one work and determined the Roman numeral assigned to the final painting.

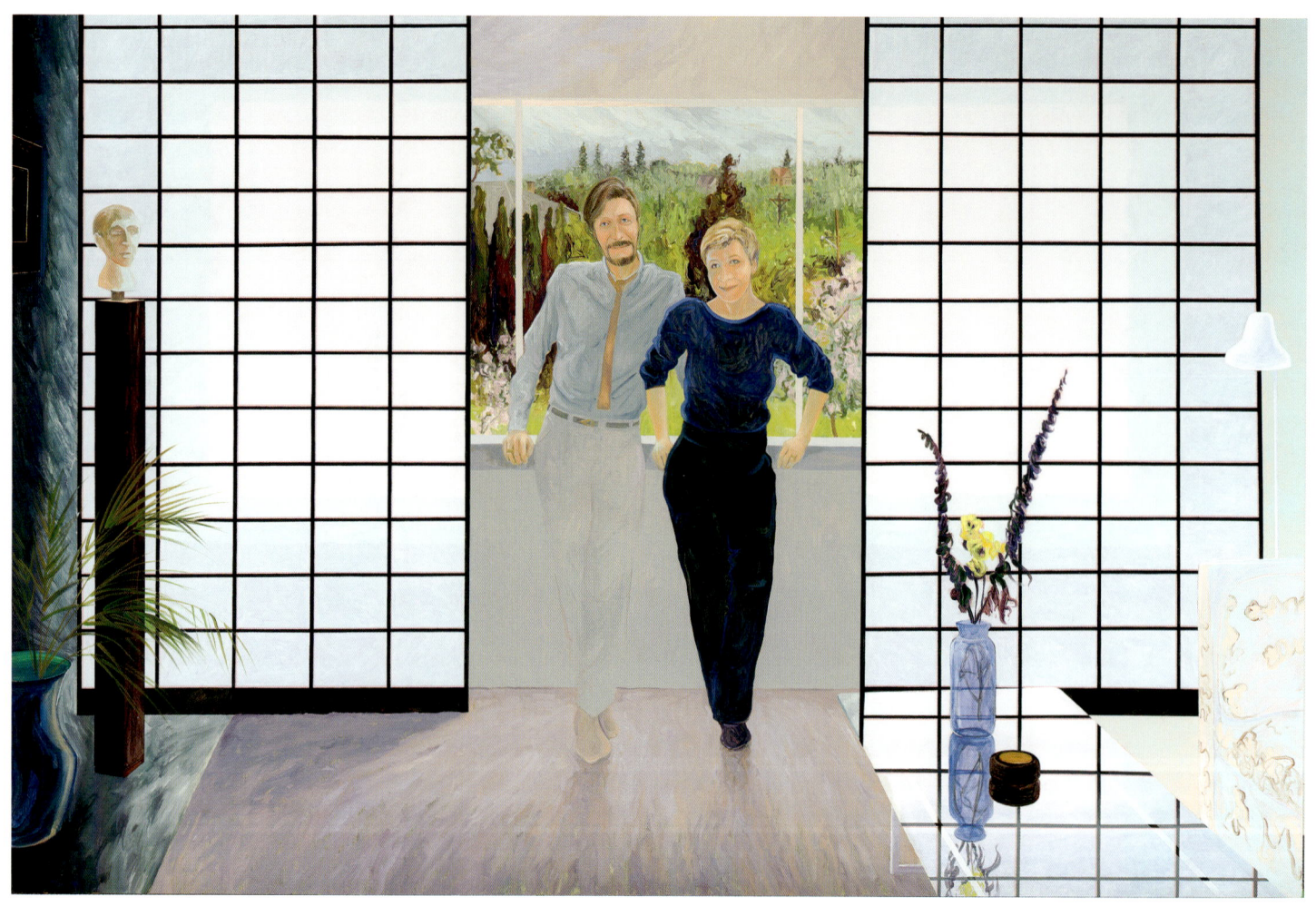

*Canadian Window #II - Victor and Barbara*, 1997-1998
oil and acrylic on canvas
66 x 100 inches (167.64 x 254 cm)

*"Barb and Vic are well known in the Victoria art scene: Barb as a painter of Victoria scenes and Vic as an illustrator and highly-skilled computer graphic artist. We became fast friends, and when it came time for Yvette and me to officially tie the knot, Barb and Vic stood up for us. We remain best friends to this day. In the painting, Vic and Barb lean upon their picture window at Windermere Place in the Fairfield area of Victoria. The shoji screens (made by Vic) filtering the outside light reflect their keen interest in Japanese culture."*

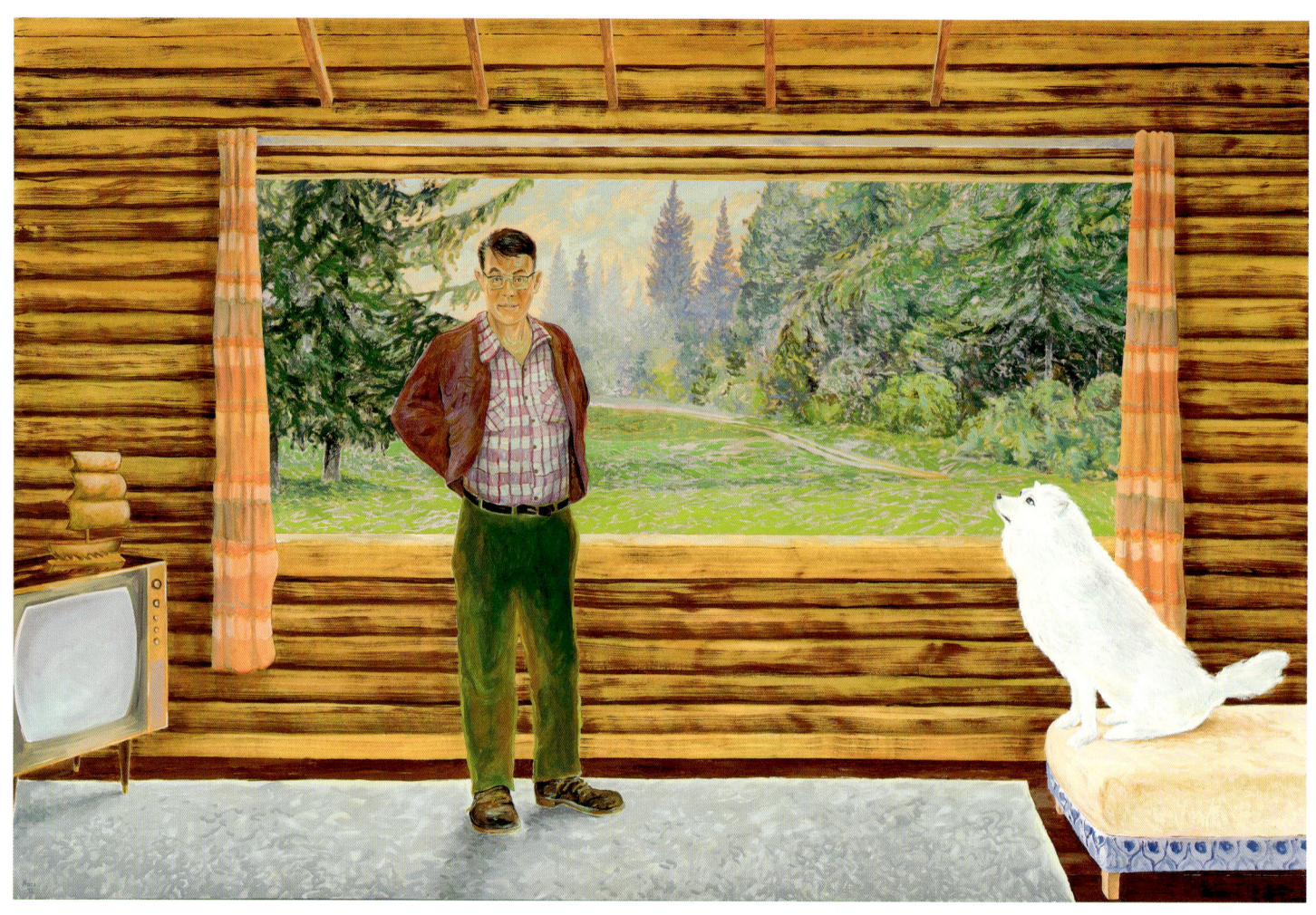

*Canadian Window #IV – Roy and Sheba*, 2012
oil and acrylic on canvas
66 x 100 inches (167.64 x 254 cm)
*Canadian Window #IV – Roy and Sheba*, 2012 on page 82

*"Roy is a fascinating character with a rather unique background. At the outbreak of the Second World War, a number of young English orphans were shipped overseas to Canada to escape the pending dangers and to receive a chance at an education. At the age of about 5 or 6 years, Roy arrived at Fairbridge Farm School just outside of Duncan, B.C. About ten years ago, Roy received contact from someone in England who turned out to be his younger sister. She had found Roy when researching her family and found out that their parents had sent him away for his protection and had lost track of him through the tumult of war. Roy was reunited with his new-found sister and was able to meet his other siblings in England. He continues to live in his cottage above Mill Bay (Vancouver Island)."*[5]

*Canadian Window XI – Michael*
(Red Deer, AB) 2000-2003
oil and acrylic on canvas
66 x 76 inches (167.64 x 193.04 cm)

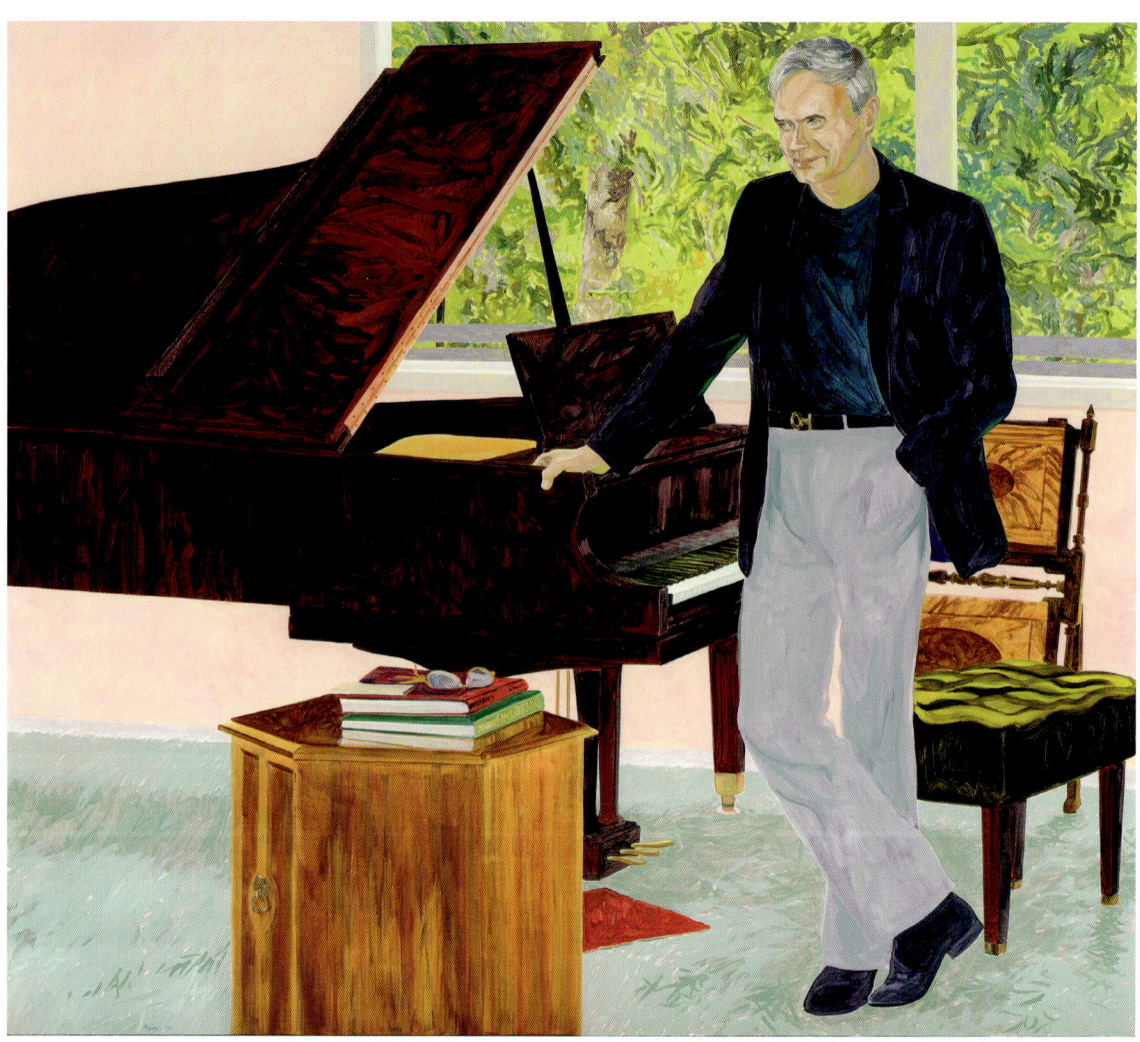

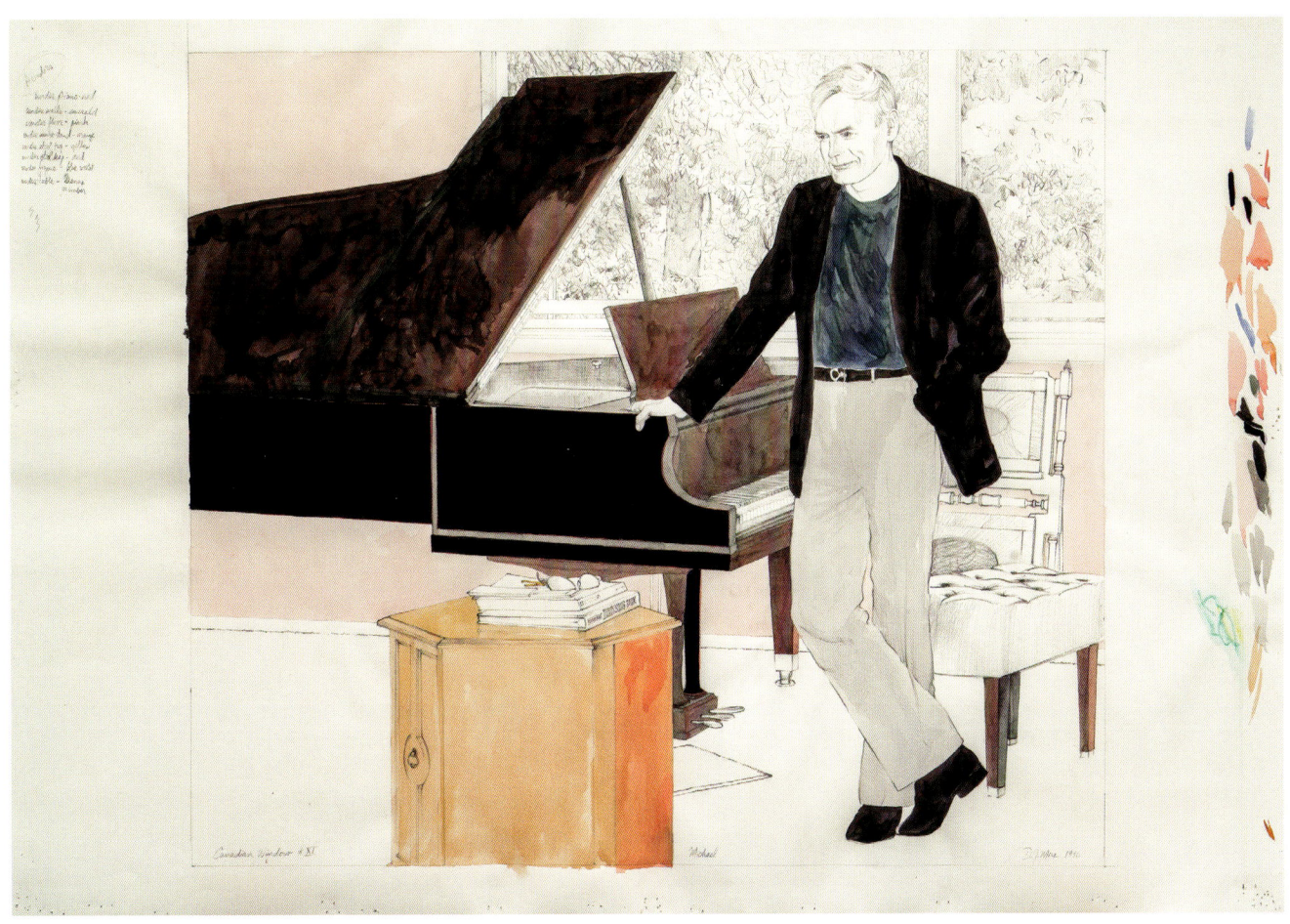

*Canadian Window XI – Michael* (*Study*), 1996
graphite, ink, watercolour on paper
26 x 30 inches (66.04 x 76.2 cm)

*Canadian Window XIII – Rod & Linda & Grizz*, 1995
graphite on paper
32 x 28 inches (81.28 x 71.12 cm)

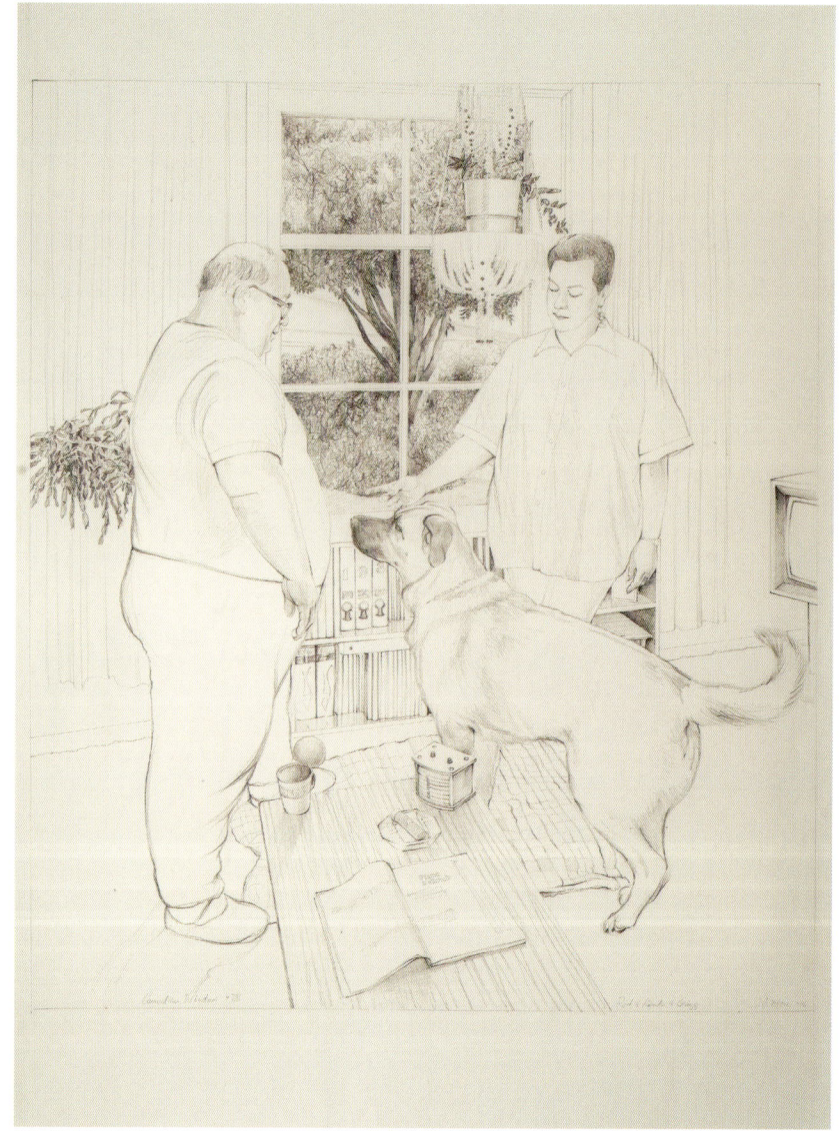

*"Rod and Linda Perks were among the first people we met when we moved to Benalto. They lived at the far end of town…two blocks away…and had a very large dog named Grizz. When a large dog showed up as a stray at our house in the cold of January, we were determined to keep him, and they gave us good advice to take care of Chummy properly. We became good friends and over the years visited back and forth."*[6]

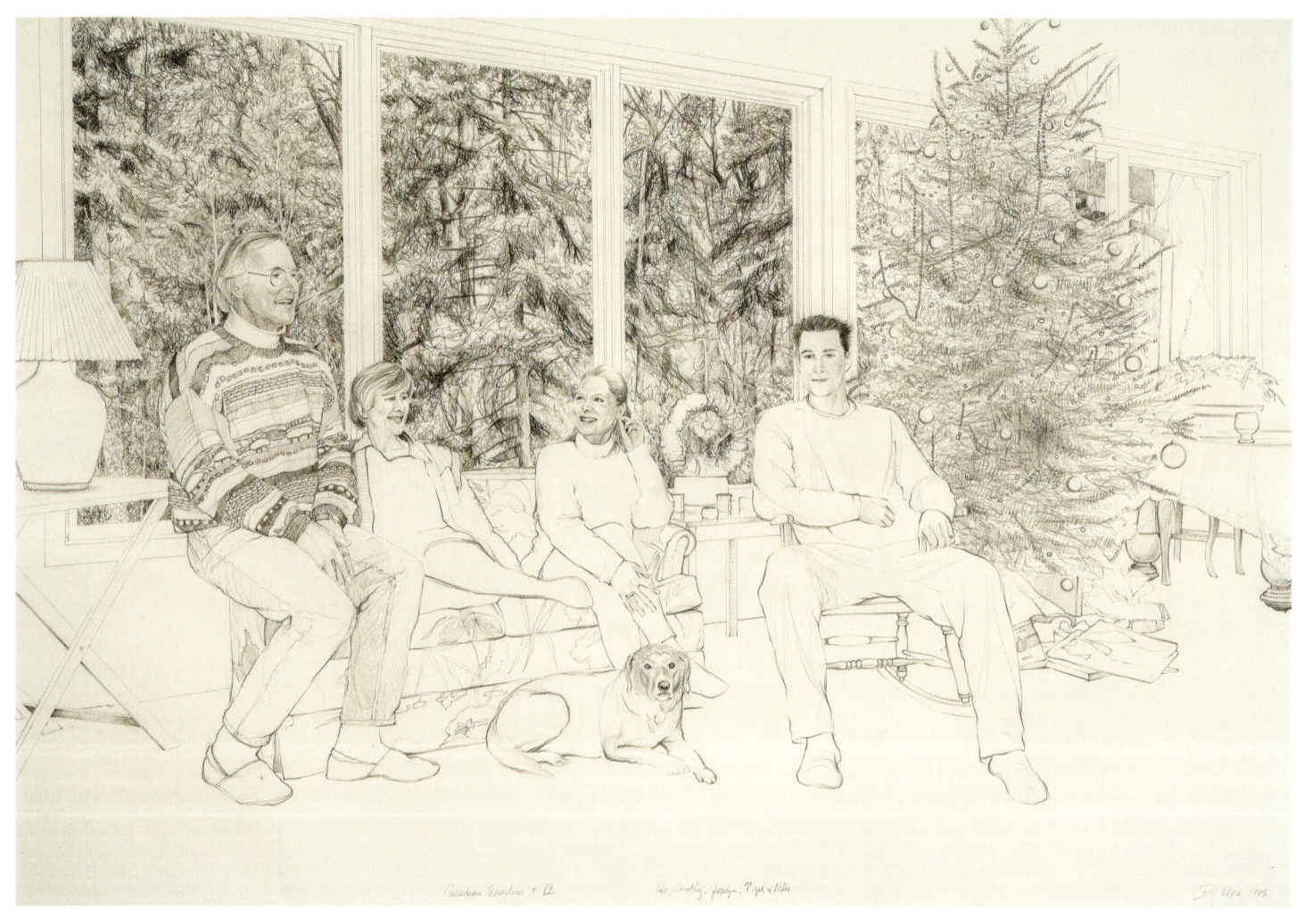

*Canadian Window IX – Tim, Dorothy, Jocelyn, Nigel, Allie* (*Study*), 1995
graphite on paper
28 x 42.5 inches (71.12 x 107.95 cm)

Four paintings complete our passage through the artist's forty-year practice. Two of them were sparked by the sight of New Brunswick's northern shoreline on the Gulf of St. Lawrence, while thousands of miles away, not far from the artist's Benalto home, it was the local resort of Sylvan Lake which inspired the other two. Key to these four artworks was the opportunity for More to try two things unexpected of a landscape artist: one involving the relationships with family and friends over time, as in *Seven Women and the Sea*, and the other melding art history with the crowded *Shore Figures* of Sylvan Lake.

The New Brunswick-based paintings began in 1985 with *Seven Women and the Sea* when two family photographs ignited the first concept drawings. Not completed as a painting until 2014, its final composition was shaped by the passage of time. Two of the seven women, Agathe and Judy, were by then deceased, so More portrays them outside a window. At the table were the living: Susan, Marie, Colette, and Yvette. In this narrative, Yvette was also portrayed on a deserted beach photographing the stormy Bay de Chaleur. It evokes time-travel and, along with *Three Men of Acadia,* features lives shaped by culture, history, and, most of all, the ever-present sea.

Around Sylvan Lake, the waters are much calmer, but on a hot summer's day the shoreline is a different matter. For More, the challenge was to cast his *Shore Figures* back into art history. Leisure-time as an activity was available in the nineteenth-century only to the bourgeoisie, as in the elegant picnic of Édouard Manet's famous *Le Déjeuner sur l'herbe* (1863), but now everyone can enjoy it, no matter what their age, income, or occupation, as More depicts in *Looking for Édouard.* In *Venus & The Biker,* a woman in a loud polka-dot bikini emulates the distinctive *contrapposto* pose of the iconic Ancient Greek statue known as *Venus de Milo* (100-130 BCE). With her back to us, this contemporary "Venus" is in lively contrast to the biker in black clothing. Sylvan Lake, Alberta, represents if nothing else an egalitarian landscape about leisurely Canadians today.

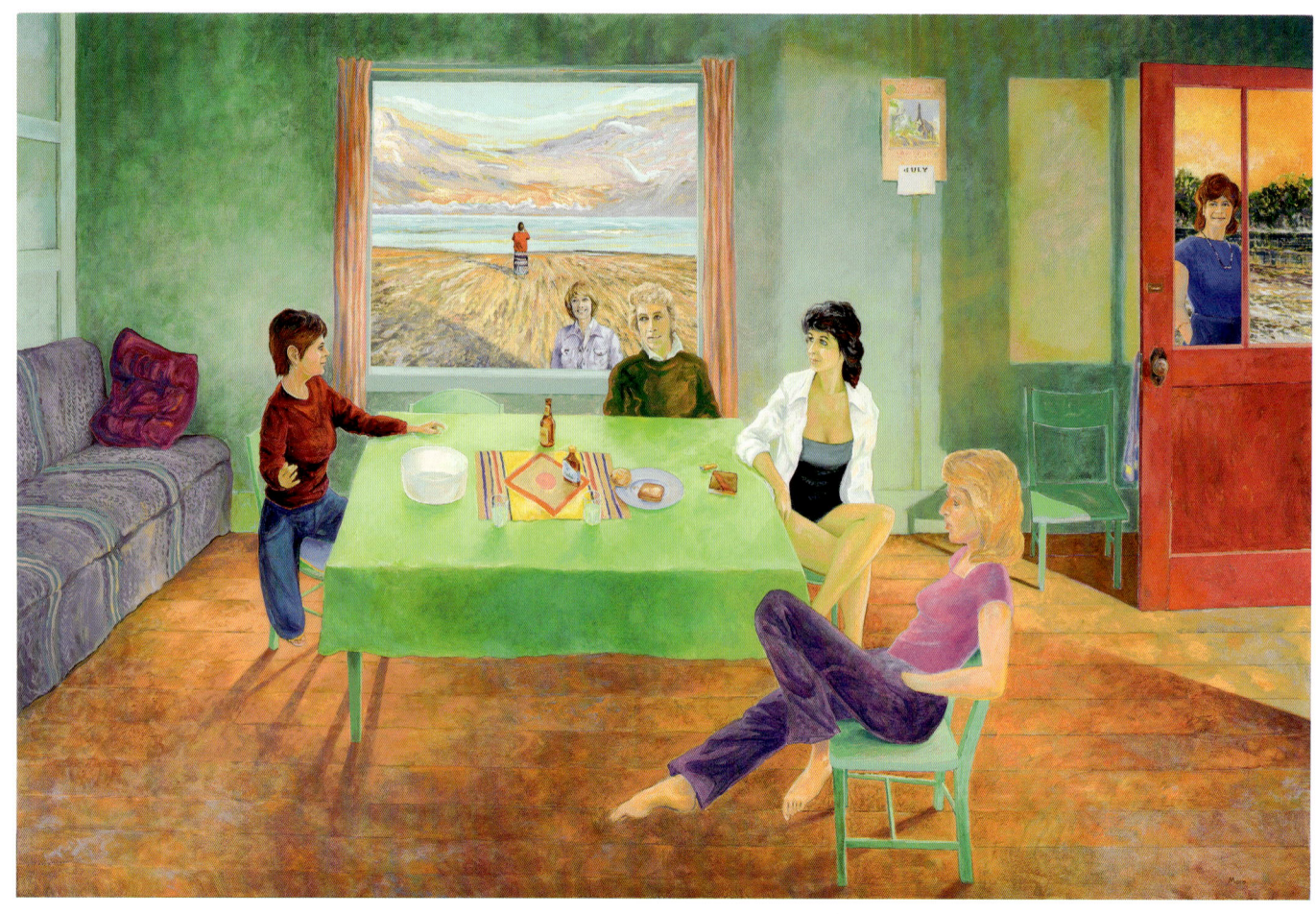

*Canadian Window I – Seven Women and the Sea – Yvette & Judy & Sue & Marie & Colette & Agathe*, 1985/1998/2014
oil and acrylic on canvas
66x 100 inches (167.64 x 254 cm)

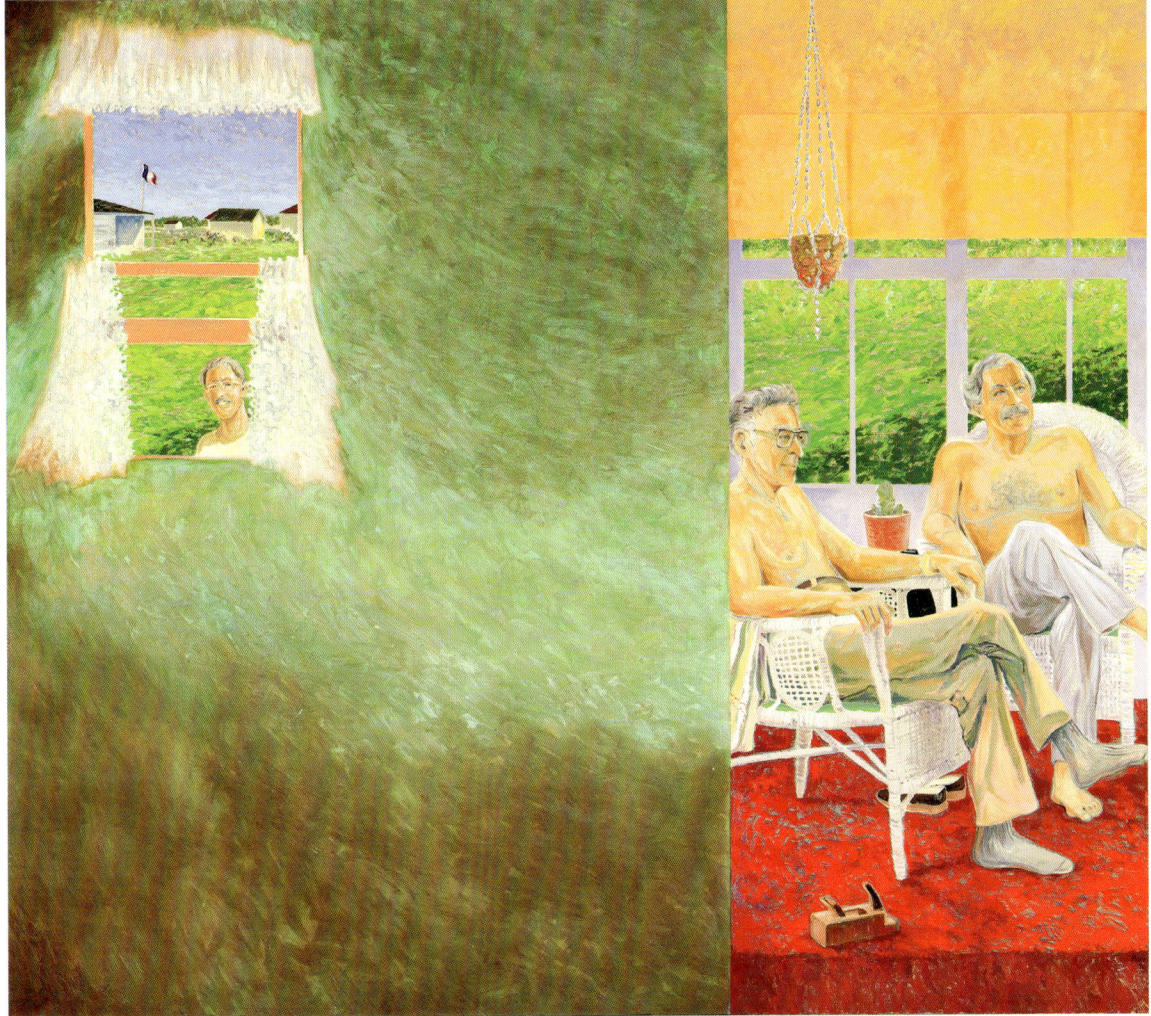

*Canadian Window X – Three Men of Acadia – Aurèle, Armand & Hilaire*, 2012
oil on canvas
66 x 75.6 inches (167.64 x 193.024 cm)

*Shore Figures, Sylvan Lake – Venus & The Biker*,
2015
oil on canvas
60 x 59.5 inches (152.4 x 151.13 cm)
Collection of the Artist

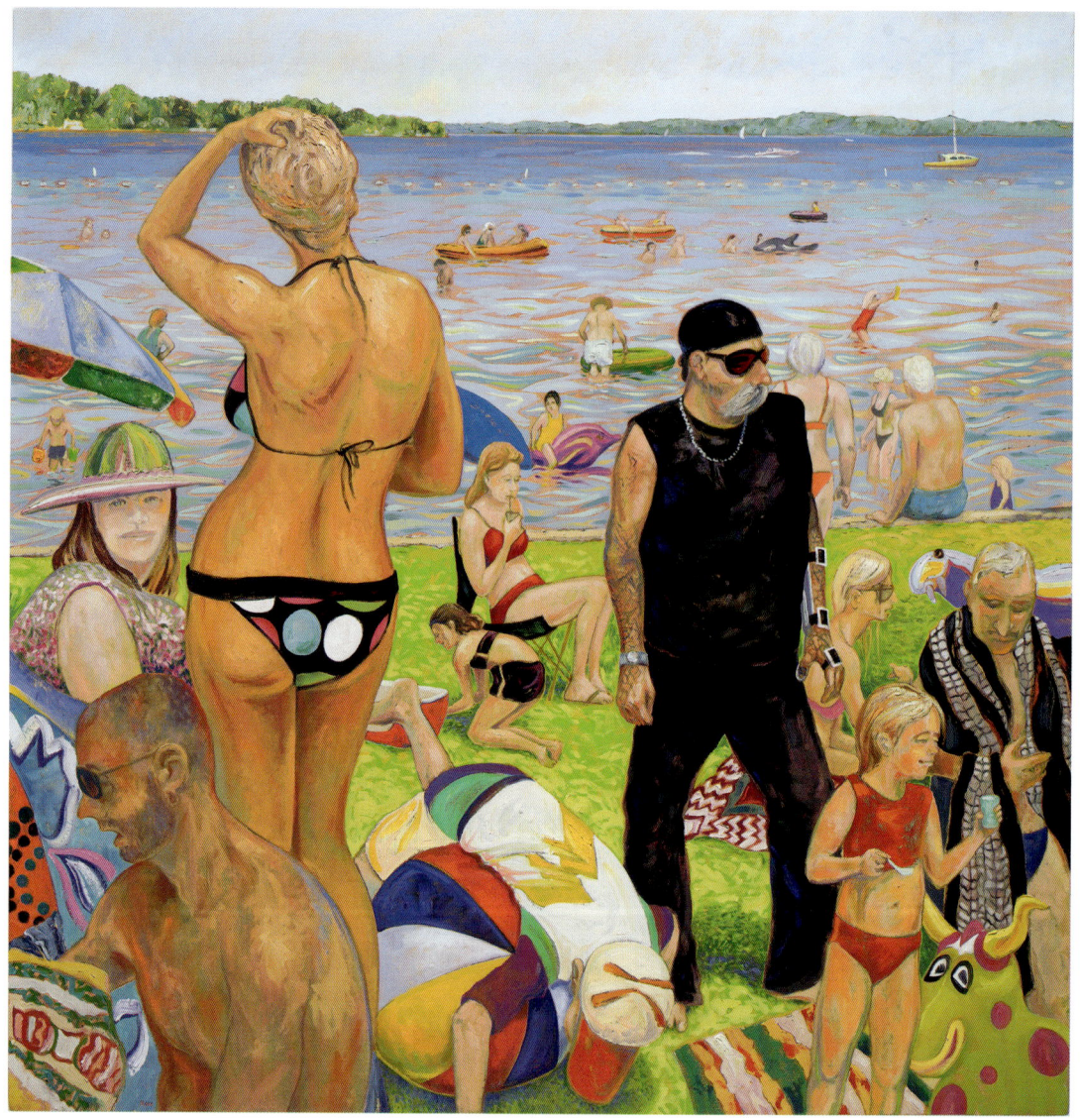

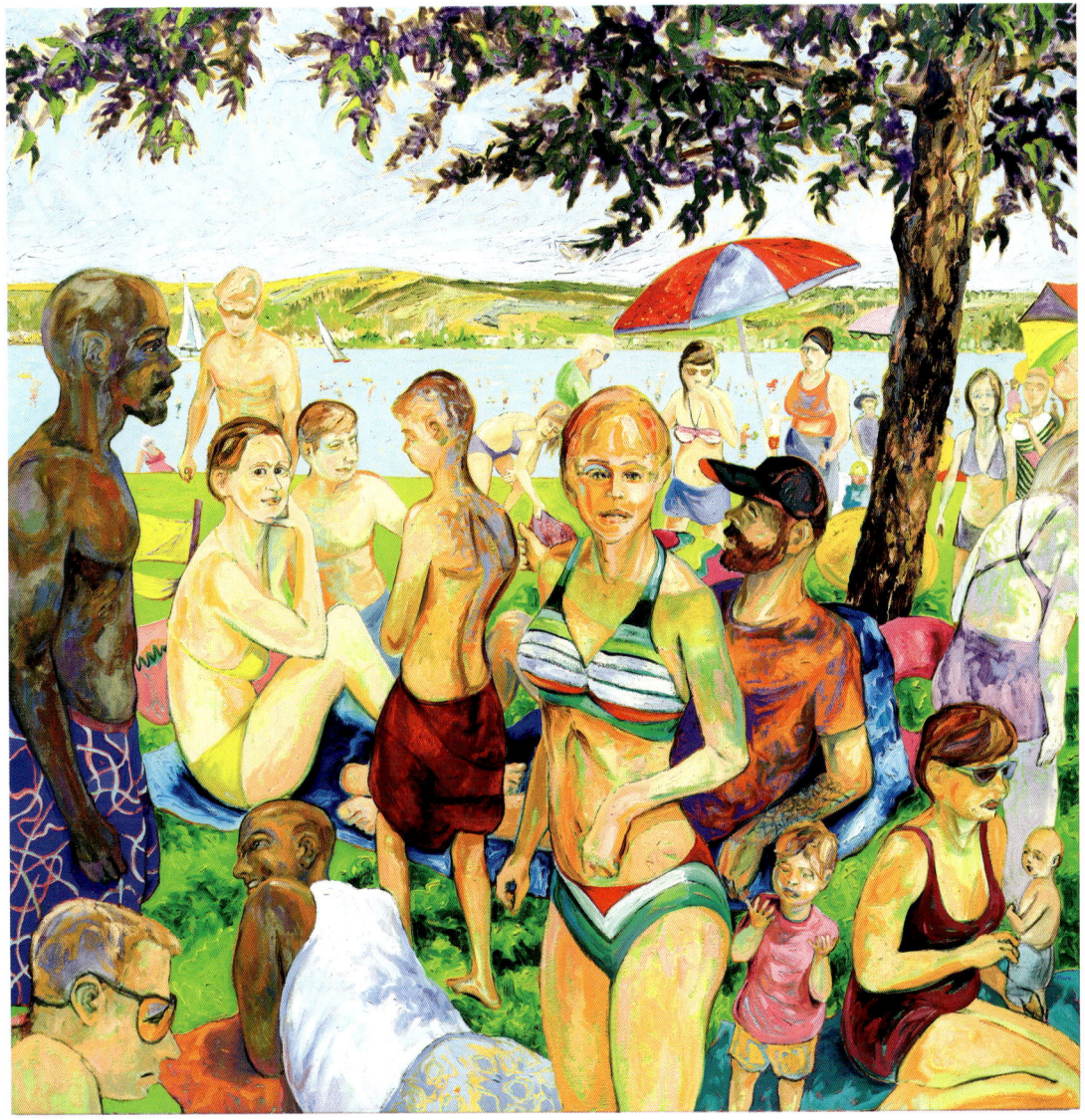

*Shore Figures, Sylvan Lake – Looking for Edouard*, 2015
oil on canvas
60 x 59.5 inches (152.4 x 151.13 cm)
Collection of the Artist

On p. 100: Detail of *Escarpment* (central Alberta), 2010 – see p. 60.

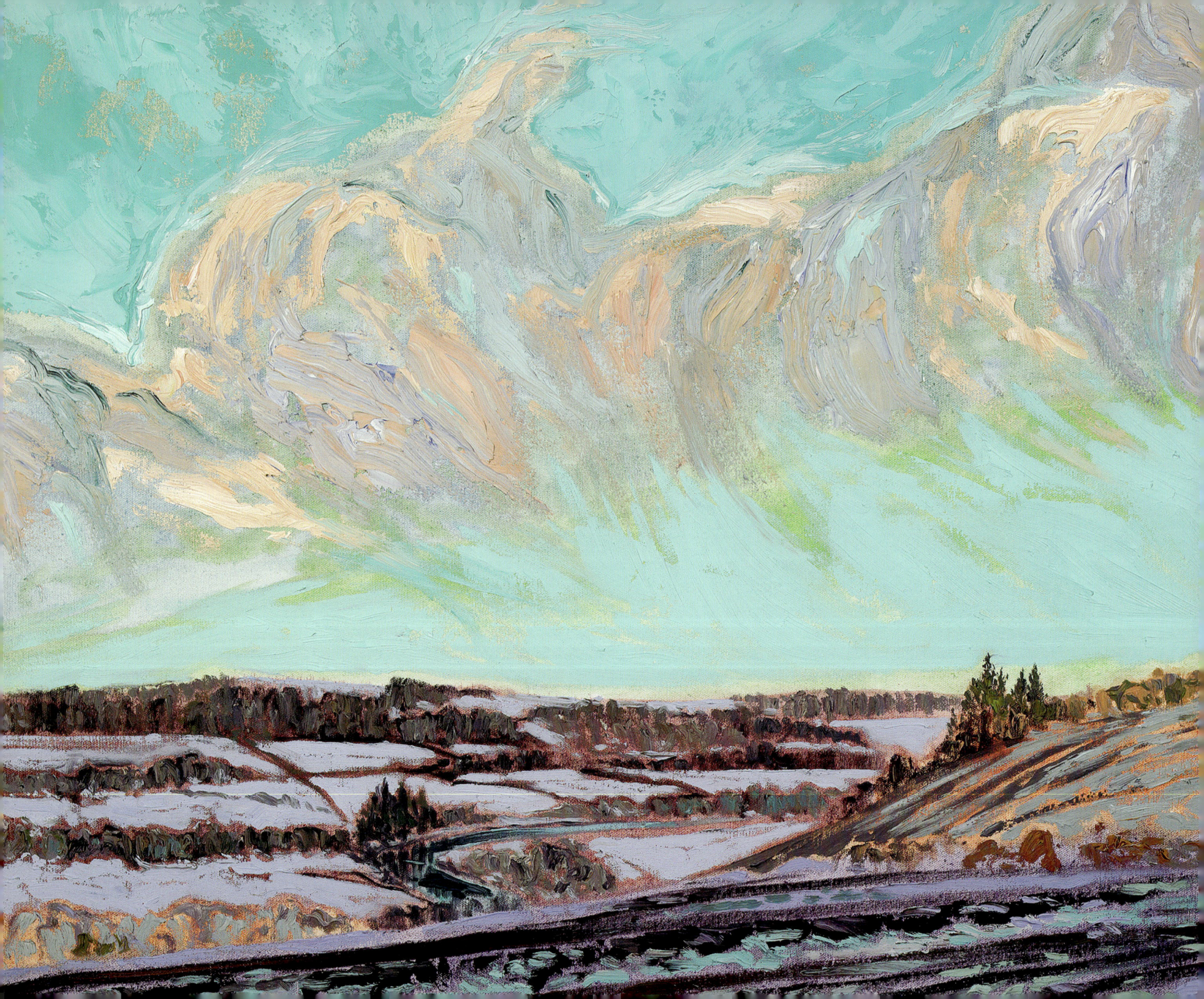

## Epilogue

At the beginning of this exploration, the artist asks us to consider ourselves "guests of this *greatest garden.*" As the paintings reproduced in this book show, he certainly makes good on this invitation. With a forty-year-plus career as a professional artist, David More has always been intent on making the best of his training and skills as a painter. In return, the greatest garden–as he relates to it–has not diminished in importance. There is still an immense 'landscape' out there to reckon with, whether wild or cultivated, uninhabited or crowded with people, such those as on the Sylvan Lake beaches.

Maybe, in the future, there will be further trips to northern New Brunswick or elsewhere, giving him new insights. In the meantime, David More has created a large and meaningful body of work with several chapters, reflected in the chapters of this book. In each, a certain subject has been brought to light, some poetic and metaphorical as in *The Garden Ceremony* and *War's Garden*, others more direct in their meaning, such as the Acadian forests silenced by environmental degradation or the powerful skies above central Alberta alluding to uncertain weather and climate change.

Unusual for a landscape artist has also been the attention he has paid to the human presence, incorporated as a subject within the greater garden which we all inhabit. What of that personal and private place called Benhaven? Painted so directly and intuitively by a master of the plein air, from this tiny refuge on the planet, with strong colour, painterly means, and rich compositions veering towards the abstract, David More gives us a place to begin.

## NOTES TO INTRODUCTION

1   David More, "Artist Biography and Statement," *Chinook Christmas: Illustrations by Dave More*. Exhibition brochure, Red Deer & District Museum, October 24 to November 21, 1993.

2   Ibid.

3   More graduated with a Diploma in Painting in 1972.

4   Exhibited a year later after graduation.

5   The elegant six-storey Burns Building, built by cattle baron Pat Burns is still standing today across from Olympic Plaza as an historic site. The artist studios along with the Burns Visual Arts Society are located today in the Ramsay neighbourhood of Calgary.

6   Studio notes on Process by David More. Transcribed for the author in 2020.

7   Ibid.

8   The summertime workshops were suspended in 2012.

9   See exhibition catalogue, *The Flat Side of the Landscape: The Emma Lake Artists' Workshops,* edited by art historian John O'Brian (Saskatoon: Mendel Art Gallery, 1989).

10  Ibid, p. 141-44

11  Between 1983-1995, the artist completed six outdoor mural commissions in Chemainus, BC, Welland, Ontario, and Bashaw, Stony Plain, Fort Macleod, and Sylvan Lake, Alberta.

12  See Patricia Ainslie's excellent book, *Okanagan Artists in their Studios* (Calgary: Frontenac House, 2013).

## NOTES TO CHAPTER 1

1   Transcription of More studio notes given to author, 2020.

2   Ibid.

## NOTES TO CHAPTER 2

1   Transcription of More studio notes given to author, 2020.

2   Exhibition brochure published by Paul Kuhn Gallery (Calgary, 1999), p. 5.

3   Ibid.

## NOTES TO CHAPTER 3

1   Transcription of Interview with Mark Weber.

2   Mark Weber, "Fade to Silent," *The Advocate* (Red Deer, AB), July 27, 1991).

3   Jason Proctor, "Adding a tragic chapter to the legacy of Canadian art," *Medicine Hat News*, June 26, 1992.

4   Transcription of More studio notes given to author, 2020.

5   Mary-Beth Laviolette, Curator. Panel text for exhibition, October 12, 2019–January 1, 2020.

## NOTES TO CHAPTER 4

1   Transcription of More studio notes given to author, 2020.

2   *The Garden Ceremony*, published by artist (2010), p. 5.

3   *…of Gardens*, published by artist (September 29, 1996) p. 1.

4   *The Garden Ceremony*, published by artist (2010), p. 14.

## NOTES TO CHAPTER 5

1   Transcription of More studio notes given to author, 2020.

2   *Mr & Mrs Smith and Percy* is in London's Tate collection.

3   Transcription of More studio notes given to author, 2020.

4   Susan Delaney. "The Painter's Gift: A show drawn from works donated by the Alberta Artist reveals unexpected investigations," *GalleriesWest* (November 21, 2019).

5   Ibid.

6   Ibid.